PREFACE

Recently the media has brought to the attention of the public many horror stories on the sensitive topic of poor nursing home care. This is not a new problem; the United States Senate Special Subcommittee on Aging had held many workshops attended by experts in the geriatric field, all trying to improve the level of care in nursing homes. The federal government has already enacted a sweeping reform by passing the Omnibus Budget Reconciliation Act (OBRA) of 1987, imposing stricter regulations on the nursing home industry. State inspectors have followed by increasing the number of citations on numerous deficiencies, by levying fines, and even by shutting down or taking away the licenses of nursing home operators. Yet the care for the residents has not appreciably improved. There are still tales of abuse and neglect occurring across the country. It is no wonder that placing a loved one into a nursing home is often a heart-wrenching decision. It is a traumatic time for both the one to be placed and the one who is considering placement of a loved one.

You already have access to a great many books and pamphlets from various consumer organizations and libraries on how to choose a nursing home. However, none of these sources provide you with the type of information and insight I am prepared to give you. Using my combined nursing and social work experience and background, my goals are: (1) to provide you with an idea of what you can and should expect from nursing home staff personnel, and how you can participate in your loved one's day-to-day "activities of daily living" (ADL); (2) to inform you and your loved one that you have the law and the rights behind you totally. Do not let the facility intimidate you into not filing complaints when the need is there. Equipped with the knowledge of the law and how the facilities operate, you can become an informed and powerful consumer advocate. By your active involvement you can protect your loved one as well as all other nursing home residents from being mistreated, neglected or abused.

You can use this book as a practical guide both before and after you have placed your loved one in a nursing home. **Chapter one** provides you with information on which way to turn when you are making the crucial decision on placement. **Chapter two** contains a historical background of nursing homes in America, leading up to the new regulations currently in force with which every facility in the country must comply. **Chapter three** discusses the different types of facilities, their ownership, the staff personnel and their responsibilities. **Chapter four** contains questions and observations to use in choosing one nursing home over another. **Chapter five** covers information you should know regarding the process of admitting your loved one into a facility, and if need be, to transfer out. **Chapter six** deals with the question of financing the nursing home stay, including information on Medicare, Medicaid, and private insurance. The next four chapters all deal with residents' rights. I will clarify what constitute deficiency, abuse, mistreatment, and neglect. **Chapter seven** discusses the desired level of quality of life. **Chapter eight** provides insight on the quality of care and how to improve it. **Chapter nine** deals specifically with chemical restraints and how to prevent excessive use of these pharmacological agents. **Chapter ten** discusses physical restraints and how to prevent the excessive use of this type of restraint. An important question that I will answer for you is, "What are some of the alternative measures for my loved one before physical or chemical restraints are prescribed?" **Chapter eleven** lists some of the significant problems of nursing homes, and how you as an informed consumer can help in resolving them.

The nursing home industry is a service provider. When the owner/administrator realizes that you are knowledgeable about nursing home regulations, that you know how to get in touch with the appropriate people when you do not get satisfaction from them, and that you anticipate and try to resolve potential problems before an incident of abuse or neglect actually occurs, he or she will strive to improve the quality of life and quality of care for your loved one within his or her facility.

I am an ardent believer that by arming yourself with the knowledge you acquired from this book, and by your active participation in the enforcement of existing regulations, positive changes will take place in the nursing home industry. The benefits derived for all residents, will be "to attain or maintain the highest practical level of physical, mental, psychosocial and spiritual well being." This is the primary goal of the Omnibus Budget Reconciliation Act of 1987. This in turn will make the decision to place a loved one into nursing home easier for all of us facing such a dilemma.

Elizabeth T. Yeh
RN, BSN, MSW
Davis, California
March 31, 1995

ACKNOWLEDGMENT

This book is dedicated to my mother, whose independence and indomitable spirit inspired me to always strive for the utmost best. Alas, at ninety-one, she is much too young for the topic of this book. I am sincerely thankful to Dr. Norman Roth, my former professor from the California State University, Sacramento, School of Social Works, who graciously offered to spend his spare time editing and giving constructive criticism about this book. I also thank my social work colleague and friend, Eunice Gates, who spent hours on the phone talking to me about the contents of this book. I am very appreciative of all my friends who have shown their unwavering support over the past year.

During the writing of this book my family has given me constant support, reassurance, and encouragement. My parents-in-law helped to inspire me, especially my father-in-law, even in times of his failing health. To them, I am forever indebted. To my older daughter, Debra, who took time from her busy medical practice to meticulously correct and edit my manuscript, I am eternally grateful for her persistence, thoroughness, and dedication. To my younger daughter, Tamara, I thank her for her knack of always knowing when I am discouraged and frustrated, and for being there to encourage me when my spirits are down. To my husband of thirty-four years, Yin, my deepest love and gratitude go to him. He has continuously giving me motivation, and his endless patience, skills and wisdom. Finally, I like to thank my publisher, Mr. Edward Rosenwasser, for giving me this chance to make my dream come true.

TABLE OF CONTENTS

Preface   *i*
Acknowledgment   *iv*
Table of Contents   *v*
Abbreviations   *vi*

1. The Crucial Decision   1
2. An Overview of
   Long-Term Care Facilities   13
3. Nursing Home Types   31
4. Choosing a Nursing Home   45
5. Admission and Transfer   58
6. Financing Nursing Home Care   76
7. Quality of Life   97
8. Quality of Care   117
9. The Use of Chemical Restraints   134
10. Physical Restraints   155
11. Problem Areas and
    Potential Solutions   170
Addendum   192
Bibliography   197
Glossary   206
Resources   215
Index   220

ABBREVIATIONS

ADL---Activities of Daily living
B/B --- Bowel and Bladder
BM --- Bowel movement
BOD --- Board of Directors
CNA--- Certified Nursing assistant
COPD --- Chronic obstructive pulmonary disease
CPR--- Cardio-pulmonary resuscitation
CVA--- Cerebrovascular accident
DHS--- Department of Health Services
DON--- Director of Nurses (or Nursing)
DRG--- Diagnosis Related Group
DSD--- Director of Staff Development
ECF --- Extended care facility
G/T tube--- Gastrostomy tube
HCFA--- Health Care Financing Administration
HEW--- Department of Health, Education and Welfare
HHA--- Home Health Agency or Home Health Aide
HHS--- Department of Health and Human Services
ICF---Intermediate Care Facility
IV--- Intravenous fluid line
LOA--- Leave of Absence
LVN--- Licensed Vocational (Practical) Nurse
M.D.--- Physician; Doctor
MDS--- Minimum Date Set
MRQ --- Medicare Review Questionaire
MSW--- Medical Social Worker
N/G tube--- Nasogastric tube
NA--- Nursing Assistant
O2 tube---Oxygen tube (Nasal cannula)
OAA--- Old Age assistance
OBRA--Omnibus Budget Reconciliation Act of 1987
OT--- Occupational Therpist

PASARR----Pre-Admission Screening and Annual Resident
     Review
PCC--- Patient Care Coordinator
PMR --- Physician's medical records (MD's order sheet)
POE --- Medicaid billing number card
PPD --- TB skin test
PSC ---Professional Service Consultant
PSS --- Professional Service Specialist
PT--- Physical Therapist
RA --- Rehabilitative or restorative aide
RAI--- Resident Assessment Instrument
RAPS --- Resident Assessment Protocal
RN--- Registered Nurse
ROM---- Range of Motion
SNF--- Skilled Nursing Facility
ST--- Speech Therapist
STAT --- Immediately
URC---Utilization Review Committee

CHAPTER 1

The Crucial Decision:
To Nursing Home or Not, With Love

After the Initial Shock...3
Looking into the Options...4
The Home Care Option...7
Serious Consideration of the Nursing Home Option 10

One beautiful Sunday afternoon, you and your family are sitting around a table playing cards, joking and laughing. Suddenly you notice that one of your loved ones cannot speak or move one side. Her eyes roll backward into her head. Her breathing is not normal. She does not respond when you call her name. Frantically you dial 911 within a short time the fire department personnel and the ambulance paramedics arrive. You are requested to step aside without any explanation. Many questions are fired at you by the paramedics in rapid fashion, all in strange medical jargon. You do not understand what many of these words mean. One paramedic is talking to someone on the phone and you have no idea to whom he is speaking. Another proceeds to unbutton your loved one's shirt and starts to attach some strange gadgets onto her chest. A tube is put into her nose. They also insert something into her mouth. Some sort of fluid is running into her arm. You are petrified with all these strange things that are happening to your loved one. The next thing you know, the paramedics are placing your loved one onto a narrow gurney (stretcher) and preparing to take her to the emergency room of the nearest hospital. They tell you to meet them there.

With a throbbing heart and the fear that a catastrophic illness has befallen your loved one, you arrive at the hospital's emergency room. Immediately, you hear various strange sounds coming from the many machines behind the curtained cubicles. You are very anxious, apprehensive, frustrated, and your fear is becoming unbearable. All of a sudden, you have been thrown into another new and strange world. The hospital staff also speak a different language, using more medical jargon that you do not understand when they speak with you. People are running around, some wearing uniforms or white coats, while others are in street clothes. You stand there not knowing where to turn, to whom to speak, or even where your loved one is located. Then you hear your name being called, and you are led into a room where your loved one is lying on another narrow gurney. She looks lifeless and pale. Upon a closer look you notice one tube is going into her nose with two short prongs in her nostrils; this tube (*the oxygen tube*) goes across her face and behind her ears. One more tube is attached in her arm (*the intravenous line*); another strange gismo is attached on her index finger (*measuring pulse and oxygen saturation rate*). Still another tube is coming from beneath the sheet and attached to a bag that hangs under the gurney (*indwelling Foley catheter for collecting urine*). Horrible thoughts of the unthinkable are swirling in your head; no one is there to take the time to explain to you why they are doing these things. Then a total stranger in a white coat walks in and assures you that your loved one now is in a stable condition. You find out later that the person who spoke to you is the emergency room doctor. After the preliminary examinations, this doctor and your own family doctor finally tell you that your loved one will have to be admitted to the hospital for further tests and observation. After another waiting period the transporter comes and transfers your loved one either to the intensive care unit or to a regular floor. On the floor, the physician who ordered the numerous tests comes to tell you that your loved one had a cerebrovascular accident (CVA or stroke), and her right side has been paralyzed by the CVA. The physician further assured you that your family member has made it through this initial acute stage. Her condition is still serious but stable.

This story, though fictional, will strike a familiar note with many. Unfortunately, so will the remainder of this story. For overcoming the acute stage of a severe, debilitating illness usually does not mean that everything will return to normal.

All patients admitted to an acute hospital must comply with the Diagnosis Related Group (DRG) guidelines, outlining how many days Medicare will pay for their inpatient stay ordered by the physician. This number is based on a standard formula: the nature of the illness, its severity, the general condition of the patient, and the normal stay period for someone with this condition.[1] This guideline will help the staff to determine the estimated number of days that the patient will be in the acute hospital. Patient stays longer than the guideline will result in the hospital absorbing the monetary loss. In principle, this guideline will force the hospital to work hard to get a patient well and send him/her home ahead of schedule.[2] Thus, discharge planning starts immediately.

---

[1]Smith, Carol E., DRGs: Making them work for you, *Nursing 85* 15: 34-41, 1985.

[2]**Diagnostic Related Groups (DRG):** This disease-treatment association is created by the federal government in its attempt to contain the skyrocketing acute hospital costs. It assumes that on the average, every patient with the same diagnosis will suffer and recover in the same way and in the same period of time. There are approximately five hundred diagnoses in the DRG index. Each diagnosis is multiplied by a weighting factor, and this weighting factor reflects a cost that is an estimate of the average cost of providing care for that diagnosis in a certain geographical area. Given a specific diagnosis, Medicare insurance (to be discussed in Chapter 6) will only pay benefits for that particular diagnosis up to an amount designated by this schedule and only for that specified time. Each patient admitted into an acute care hospital is allowed only one diagnosis per DRG admission, regardless of the true number of ailments he may suffer. It sets a certain dollar value based on

4   The Crucial Decision

Because of the DRG, as soon as your loved one is admitted onto the floor the process of planning for his/her discharge is handled by the Patient Care Coordinator (PCC). This is the time to find out who the patient care coordinator assigned to your loved one is. You should ask the PCC how many days your loved one will be expected to stay in the hospital. This will give you time to decide what you want to do after his/her discharge. At the same time, you should obtain all the written material on nursing homes and various home health agencies so that you can read them later when you feel less stressed. This will allow you time to develop pertinent questions to ask when you make the visits to these places. The big question on your mind is, "Will I be able to care for my loved one at home immediately after discharge or will I have to put my loved one into a nursing home?"

No one really seriously thinks about nursing homes until a catastrophic illness impairs a loved one. While your loved one is in the hospital, the doctor, the patient care coordinator and the rehabilitation team members will give you an honest evaluation of the recovery period and the effort that you and other members of your family will need to make during this time. If your decision is to transfer your loved one to a rehabilitation unit, either in a nursing home or in an acute hospital, the patient care coordinator will be very helpful in arranging transportation and bed for your loved one before the day of his/her discharge. The PCC will also discuss with you the other alternative: going home and using home health agency services.

Among the many terms used to describe long-term care facilities are nursing homes, convalescent hospitals, and

---

the diagnosis, to be paid in advance to hospitals that provide acute care services. After that expenditure, Medicare will spend no more money for that particular patient with that particular DRG. Unfortunately, DRG is not concerned with the ultimate fate of any one person, or even of a population. It is only concerned with how its funds (Medicare) are used in the immediate present.

skilled nursing facilities. In actuality they mean the same thing. These terms will be used interchangeably in this book.

A skilled nursing facility (SNF) means that the facility is licensed and certified both by the Federal and the State governments to participate in Medicare and Medicaid programs. Usually, the SNF part of a facility constitutes only a small part of the total nursing home beds. This unit is primarily geared towards providing an accelerated medically reasonable and necessary services, active skilled nursing care and rehabilitation services on a daily basis. These services are under direct supervision of the physician. The patient/resident must meet the stringent Medicare guideline criteria which will be discussed in Chapter 6. For someone who is being discharged after a stroke, as in our example, this will be the component of the nursing home in which she will be placed.

We all realize that when the elderly get sick, they are generally more sick than those of younger age. When they are hospitalized, they are likely to have multiple diagnoses resulting from serious ailments. Their average length of stay in a hospital is longer than that of the younger patients. Their recovery period also takes longer. Unfortunately, with an increasing focus on reducing medical costs through shorter hospital stays, the elderly patients are transferred to facilities of a lower level of care or sometimes to their own homes much sooner than before, frequently long before the illness is completely stabilized. As a result, the DRG-motivated plan has evolved into a revolving door for the older and frail elderly while the hospitals cash in on a short-term windfall. With an influx of these complicated and sicker residents, most of the nursing homes are not equipped to handle them. Uncontrolled and unforeseenable medical, nursing and social problems develop, and these residents are often sent back to the acute hospital, sometimes within hours after arrival, other times within a day. Seizing upon this opportunity, contemporary nursing home facilities are beginning to diversify their services by setting up distinct Medicare skilled nursing units to facilitate this demand.

At the time of the discharge planning conference, the patient must be informed of all the options. You must talk to your loved one with honesty and with a clear explanation of the reason why nursing home placement may be one of the options. You then need to wait for a full response from your loved one. You need to realize that when a person is being uprooted or otherwise informed that something traumatic will happen to his/her life, such as being placed in a nursing home, he/she will go through a period of grief and "mourning" as part of the adjustment. The period may be very brief or it can extend for a long time, depending on the individual.

There are five stages of grief that your loved one may go through[3]: <u>Denial</u> - the "no, not me" stage. Family members should allow the loved one some period of time to adjust to the new demands of his/her illness and the possibility of entering a nursing home. <u>Anger</u>- the "why me" stage. Your loved one may resent and show anger at anyone who is well and not in his/her predicament. He/she may even develop anger towards you for making such a suggestion as putting him/her in a nursing home. He/she may go out of his/her way to make you feel guilty. He/she will fear rejection and abandonment by family members and friends. It is important not to take this anger personally and not to become angry yourself with your loved one. He/she will complain about all sorts of things that the nursing home represents. Be sure to let him/her express his/her true feelings freely and maintain an active, sincere listening attitude. Do not argue or be judgmental toward him/her but do give him/her all the emotional support he/she needs. Strive to keep the communication lines open. <u>Bargain</u> - the

[3]Reprinted with permission from Gillogly, Barbara, <u>California Certified Nursing Assistant's Course</u>, Quality Care Health Foundation, 1988, pp.340-341.

"yes, but" stage. The inevitability of going to a nursing home is beginning to be accepted because of deteriorating medical, mental or physical conditions. However, he/she may still bargain with you, "I will promise to be good. I will try not to wet the bed. I will not be too demanding if you let me stay at home." <u>Depression</u> - the "poor me " stage. This is the stage where reality can no longer be denied or bargained away, and your loved one will become depressed. He/she may cry or he/she may refuse to eat or drink. This is when he/she needs a great deal of tender loving care and understanding. <u>Acceptance</u> - the "yes, me" stage. Your loved one comes out of the depression and accepts the inevitable nursing home idea.

Everyone who is contemplating placing a loved one into a nursing home will have a mixed range of feelings. The difficulty in making this decision stems from feelings of confusion, disorientation, sadness, fear, frustration, anger, loneliness, embarrassment, shame, guilt, depression, doubt, helplessness, resentment, and uncertainty. All of these feelings are natural and perfectly all right.[4] As Manning stated in his book, "You must think of what your loved one needs and not what he/she wants. If love is doing what people need instead of what they want, then sometimes love must be tough."[5]

Your first collective decision may be for your loved one to go home even if the recovery phase is projected to be an extended one. In that case, you should realize that this effort could create tremendous hardships on the other family members. Often, the quality of life will decrease for everyone in the household, because the adjustments require everyone

---

[4]Richards, Marty et al., <u>Choosing a Nursing Home: A Guidebook for Families.</u> Modified and reprinted with permission from U. of Washington Press, Seattle, 1985, pp21-24.

[5]Manning, Doug, <u>The nursing home dilemma: How to make one of love's toughest decisions.</u> Reprinted with permission from In-Sight Books, Inc. and HarperCollins Publishers Inc., New York, NY, 1986, p.10.

to change, to adapt to the convalescing person, around the clock, until he/she is fully or partially recovered. There must be a relief person who will be willing and able to take over the care for a certain block of time either during the day or at night. Otherwise exhaustion sets in quickly for the sole caregiver. In the beginning your loved one will receive many telephone calls, get well cards from friends, relatives and neighbors, and each will offer various types of assistance. As time continues on, the number of calls and visits will dwindle, and soon they will disappear totally. Your loved one, you and your family will be alone to deal with this recovery phase. The speed of recovery depends on the nature of the acute illness, the motivation of your loved one to recover, and the mental/physical status at the time of discharge.

Caring for your loved one at home also may require other physical changes to be made around the house. You may have to have special bedroom furniture, i.e., a hospital bed. You may also need a bedside commode in the room, and a trapeze to be attached overhead on the bed for assistance into and out of the bed as well as for turning from side to side. The bathroom doors might also need to be widened to accommodate a wheelchair or a walker. The toilet seat may have to be raised. The bathtub needs to be readjusted to fit the sick person with a safety bar, non-skid strips and a bathing stool to prevent falls. The shower head may have to be readjusted. Meals must be cooked and prepared differently due to special dietary restrictions or difficulty in chewing and swallowing. Noise levels may have to be decreased because the convalescing person may be sleeping or resting. This is very hard on young children and teenagers. It is also very difficult to meet the physical, emotional, social, and spiritual needs of your loved one even when you provide twenty-four hours a day care for him/her. You and your family literally will not have a life of your own. You may be able to tolerate this situation for a short time, but it will take a toll on everybody in the long run.

Let us consider the home care required for a loved one who has a right-sided deficit after a stroke. He/she may also have additional impairments such as confusion, disorientation, garbled speech and incontinence of bowel/ bladder. There may be many family opinions on how best to care for such an individual. On the one hand, the physician has prescribed a rigorous rehabilitation program for your loved one, pushing him/her hard towards the road to regaining some or all of the deficits. Some family members, out of love and concern, may decide that rest and assistance for the patient is a far better cure simply because they see that the patient is more comfortable under those passive settings. These actions may translate into interference with the person who is doing the active therapy and the rehabilitation potential for that individual. Tension, conflict, and flare up develops among family members. The only way to resolve this problem is to clearly describe the reason for the goals of the rehabilitation program and the urgency for attaining these goals. If need be, these explanations have to be reinforced daily with differing levels of emphasis. The caregiver who understands the necessity of the rigorous rehabilitation program must have at least one other supportive family member to do the intervention during the conflict periods. The caregiver must have persistence and patience.

A supplement to caring at home by yourself is to have outside assistance in the form of home health care. In order to be reimbursed for home health care services, the level of care must meet Medicare guidelines. Medicare will pay for most of the supplies and durable medical equipment. These home health agencies (HHA), are certified and licensed by the Medicare program and the state to provide intermittent skilled nursing care under the direction of a registered nurse (RN), who is the coordinator for the total care of your loved one. She/he opens the case and obtains orders from the family physician to provide the following services if the need is there: physical therapy (PT), occupational therapy (OT), speech therapy (ST), Medical Social Worker (MSW) and home health aides (state certified HHAs). They will usually visit three times a week for approximately two months. The maximum time for the home health care professionals to spend in the home for each visit is one hour. The home health aide takes care of your loved one's personal care activities of daily living and cleans the immediate living area. These aides are not permitted to do heavy household chores. As a result, the rest of the time care still falls upon the family members. If you want relief and respite in home-care duties, you can request a list of names of special duty nurses and aides from the medical social worker. However, you are responsible for interviewing these private practice individuals and making the final arrangements to hire them. There are also agencies that supply homemakers. These are called Home Care or Homemaker agencies. These agencies employ and bond their employees, who come to your home to perform non-nursing duties. You will have to pay them through your private funds. At the present time, neither Medicare nor private health insurance will cover these services. Finally, after numerous discussions with the professionals, you may realize that placing your loved one in a skilled nursing facility for a short duration is unavoidable and medically necessary. Then you will start to look into the various aspects of nursing home placement.

There are both good and bad points of nursing home life. You should discuss these points completely and thoroughly with your loved one. One positive aspect of nursing home living is that a resident will be able to receive intensive daily rehabilitation services, special medical care and skilled nursing care around the clock. This will benefit those residents who are recovering from an acute illness but are still too weak to go home and are in need of rehabilitation services. Very few families are equipped to handle such intensive care at home. Another positive aspect is that there are ample opportunity for skilled nursing home residents to make new friends, to enjoy a full range of activities and to eat nutritious meals each day. They are also living in a secure, clean environment.

The negative points of living in a nursing home include: 1) Individual choices and independent decisions are limited, because the resident's livelihood is totally regimented and is established by the nursing home staff based on the needs of all residents. 2) He/she will lose his/her independence, home, spouse's companionship, daily routine, friends, social and economic status, and for some, beloved pets. For many individuals, to not have that independence is a bitter pill to swallow. He/she may even have resentment of being with all those people who are confused and disoriented if he/she feels that he/she is still alert and oriented. 3) To learn to live with a roommate who is a total stranger is another big adjustment, especially if he/she had been living alone or with his/her spouse all his/her life. As with all institutional living, the space for individual living and visiting is limited; privacy and confidentiality are rare.

In concluding this chapter, an example describing an all-too-typical situation is given. Here, it illustrates the importance of not trying to deceive a loved one into a stay in a nursing home.

An alert and oriented lady who pays for all her own medical bills was told by her family that she is going to have an x-ray taken in a hospital. In reality she is being admitted to a nursing home. When she entered the skilled nursing facility she thought she was in the acute hospital waiting to be x-rayed. The truth is that these family members did not want her to stay in their home with them anymore. They told her that they are going shopping and will be back to pick her up in a few hours. After several hours of waiting for the family, it dawned on her what was happening. She became very upset, was belligerent, combative, yelled loudly, was screaming and verbally abusive. She stated that the facility is holding her as a prisoner, demanded the use of the telephone and called all the appropriate people for help. This astute person knew her rights. With the help of the facility's Social Services Director and the cooperation of another member of her family, she was eventually transferred to an intermediate care facility. The residents in that facility are at the same level of independence as she is. This more appropriate facility is also located closer to all her friends, and they start to visit her. She in turn has adjusted to this new place without any problems and is very happy to be there. This example accentuates the importance that there must be full understanding among your loved one, your family and yourself before making the move for nursing home placement.

As you move into the following chapters, the implicit assumption that has already been made is that you and your loved one have come to a decision to have himself/herself stay in a skilled nursing facility for recuperation, rehabilitation or long-term care. This book will provide you with some of the essential know-hows for making that major transition.

CHAPTER 2

An Overview of Long-Term Care Facilities

Demographics and Perspectives...13
Historical Background..16
The OBRA Guidelines..21
The Key Elements of Resident Assessment............................24

Americans over the age of sixty-five comprise approximately 13 percent of our total population, and they are the fastest growing segment of the population. What is even more noteworthy is that those in the 75 to 85 years age group are growing at the most rapid pace! Although over 6 percent of the nation's elderly currently reside in nursing homes, this number is expected to grow as our population ages.[6] Currently, nursing home residents number about 1.5 million in our nearly 16,700 nursing homes. Statistics show about 25 percent of all people 65 and older will die in a nursing home. According to the survey results of a Special Senate Committee on Aging, the late Senator John Heinz, ranking member of that special committee,[7] the sheer demand for nursing home services will grow by almost 30 percent in the next decade, representing an increase of 7 to 9 million elderly people.

National polls consistently show that the problem of long-term care affects nearly everyone, that Americans are

[6]Reprinted with permission from Grossberg, G.T., M.D., et al., Psychiatric Problems in the Nursing Home, J. Am. Geriatrics Soc. 38: 907-917, 1990.

[7]U.S. Senate Special Committee on Aging, 101st Congress, Federal Implementation of OBRA 1987 Nursing Home Reform Provisions, Serial No. 101-4, U.S. Government Printing Office, Washington, D.C., 1990, p.38

terrified of its financial and emotional consequences, and that there is a strong and growing demand for a solution to this problem. In a survey of 1,000 registered voters conducted in July 1987,[8] 47 percent reported having had personal experience with long-term care in their own family. 14 percent had a close personal friend who had dealt with long-term care. Another 20 percent expected to have such a problem within the next 5 years. Thus fully 81 percent of registered voters had dealt with long-term care in their own family or through a close family friend, or they expected to deal with it in the near future. When most people think of long-term care, they think of older people. But actually up to 40 percent of Americans needing long-term care are under the age of 65.

In a recent *Senior Magazine* article,[9] it was reported that one of the largest group, individual and retirement insurance carriers, UNUM, commissioned the Gallup Organization to conduct a study of American attitudes about long-term disability and care. The survey interviewed 580 adults age 30 to 65. The result led the polling organization to exclaim, "Middle America's belief in their own invincibility defies reality!" Most people interviewed believe that if any long-term disability is going to happen, it is more likely to happen to the other person. In reality, men have a 43 percent chance and women have a 54 percent chance of becoming disabled during their lifetime. People underestimate by more than half the likelihood that they will become disabled at some point during their working years. People also are beginning to realize the toll of being a caregiver at home.

---

[8]McConnell, Stephen, Who Cares about Long-Term Care? *Generations*, Spring, 1990, pp 15-18. (Reprinted with permission from Generations, 833 Market Street, Suite 511, San Francisco, CA 94103. Copyright 1990, ASA).

[9]Reprinted with permission from Lang, Daphne M., Dollars & Sense, Comptalk, *Senior Magazine* - The Capitol Edition, Feb. 1994, p.16, 900 Fulton Ave. #103, Sacramento, CA 95825.

Three in ten working adults who also provide long-term care for family members say providing care hurts their family life, job and productivity. It also takes a tremendous toll in terms of emotional, physical, and psychosocial well-being. For the caregiver who has been taking care of this recovering person, exhaustion and burnout syndrome sets in. If he/she decides to get some respite help, say to attend a social gathering, rest and relaxation elude him/her because there is a constant fear that something may go wrong while he/she is away.

Nursing homes in the past had been described as "house of death, human junkyards and warehouses for the dying."[10] These patients suffered from multiple mental, physical, and emotional impairments. There was a prevalence of psychotic behavior disorders in these homes. Most of the patients were female, single, widowed, had court appointed conservators, and were on Medicaid. A 1986 survey indicated that over 60% were on public assistance.[11] Some may have lost their previous living arrangement after an acute hospitalization. Consequently, at discharge, the only choice the discharge coordinator had was to send them to a nursing home. Occasionally, they were placed into one of these facilities by their family member, because the family felt they could no longer take care of them. Often, once they were admitted, they were abandoned. That is how these homes came to have a reputation for providing long-term custodial care and services for these "patients" who we call residents now.

Even today the mere mention of nursing homes immediately conjures up many of the revolting pictures you

---

[10]Johnson, Colleen L., and Grant, Leslie A., The Nursing Home in American Society, The Johns Hopkins University Press, Baltimore, 1985, p.1

[11]Committee on Nursing Home Regulation, Institute of Medicine, Improving the Quality of Care in Nursing Homes, National Academy Press, Washington, D.C., 1986, pp.1-7

have probably seen in newspapers or on television or of stories from friends and relatives about these patients being abused and neglected by the care providers. In earlier times, visiting a patient in one of these homes could make one's stomach turn. There are strong odors all over the facility. Loud noises, anguished outbursts and cries for help permeate through the halls. Those who are up will sit in a row in the halls or in front of nursing stations with blank stares, expressionless faces and/or hanging heads. Some of them are tied to their chairs others are bound to a handle bar. Still others are kept in bed from morning until night. They have lost all incentive to fight for self-esteem, and their interest in activities or hobbies have waned into nothingness.

How is it that an industry which was developed to serve such an important function as this one became so despised and reviled in so many circles? What has the government done to redress the problems of this industry? To get a feel for this immense national problem, the many so-called efforts of the state and federal government in their attempt to regulate this industry will be reviewed.

Historical background[12]

When the federal government became involved in the regulation of nursing homes with the passage of the Social Security Act of 1935, a public assistance program for the elderly called Old Age Assistance (OAA) was established. The drafters of that legislation opposed the use of the public "poorhouse" to care for the poor elderly; the Act specifically prohibited the payment of OAA funds to residents of these types of public institutions. On the other hand, under the provisions of this Act, the establishment of private nursing homes was encouraged. The states were empowered to enforce participation and to establish standards for licensing nursing homes. However, few states were equipped to perform this important task due to lack of knowledge on

---

[12]*ibid*, Appendix A: "History of Federal Nursing Home Regulation".

specific regulations, standards and enforcement procedures. Under an environment of unclear regulations and even less defined enforcement powers, proprietary and other privately operating nursing homes flourished during that period. The industry was effectively an unregulated free enterprise.

From 1950 to 1965 several special senate committees and subcommittees were established to study the problems of the aged and aging. In 1950 amendments of the Social Security Act required the participating states to establish programs for licensing nursing homes, but it did not specify the standards or enforcement procedures. In 1959 a special committee on aging found that most of these nursing homes were substandard in quality of care, had poorly trained or untrained staff, and provided few services. In 1961 another special committee found that the inspectors of nursing homes were focusing their surveys on the physical plant rather than assessing the quality of life and the quality of care of the patients. There was no uniformity in the interpretation of regulations or in their enforcement. One facility might get a citation for a specific violation while a second facility would get only a reprimand for a deficiency of the same nature.

The year 1965 signaled the greatly expanded role of the federal government in the nursing home industry. When the Medicare and Medicaid programs were enacted, the Department of Health, Education and Welfare[13] (HEW) was given the authority to actually set federal standards for nursing homes that chose to participate in the Medicare and Medicaid programs. The Medicare Act provided funding for beneficiaries needing post-hospital convalescence in what was called an extended care facility (ECF), and Medicare

---

[13]Department of Health, Education and Welfare (HEW) has since been separated into the Department of Education and the Department of Health and Human Services (HHS). Medicare and Medicaid operate under the auspices of HHS.

paid for skilled nursing services. However, few nursing homes could meet the health and safety standards or provide levels of care for the patients as envisioned under the program. Of 6000 applicant facilities, only 740 could be fully certified. The federal government thus gave up the idea of using the ECF standards and left it up to the states to regulate the nursing home policies and enforcement.

In 1967, intermediate care facilities (ICF) came into existence. Such facilities were established so that patients who do not need twenty-four hour skilled nursing services could still be provided with more than custodial care. A licensed vocational/practical nurse would be on duty around the clock to monitor medical and nursing problems nursing assistants (NA) would help with partial or minimal care in activities of daily living. The patients of these facilities must be able to control their bowel and bladder, and be able to move around independently, with the help of a walker, cane, wheelchair, or with minimal assistance. Overall, however, the regulatory mechanisms of the states continued to be totally inadequate. Pressure to increase the standards of nursing homes that participate in Medicare and Medicaid programs and to improve their enforcement began to build in the early 1970s.

In the years 1970 and 1971, nursing home problems became front page news with a fire that killed 32 residents in Ohio and a case of food poisoning in Maryland that killed 36. However, attempts to make regulations effective suffered one setback after another. In 1972, Congress hassled with the remnants of Nixon's comprehensive welfare reform bill that included full federal funding of state surveys and certification activities. However the law also reduced the required nursing and social worker coverage in these nursing facilities.

In 1974, the Office of Nursing Home Affairs conducted a study on the quality of care in nursing homes. They found that the extent to which nursing homes comply with federal standards of care, even at that minimum level, varied widely. They also found that the inspectors looked only for the facility's capacity to deliver service rather than the true quality of care rendered. After much debate and discussion, finally in 1980, the Health Care Facilities Administration (HCFA) published its new guidelines which would (1) consolidate patient care planning to focus on the total welfare of the patients, (2) de-emphasize the medical model of care (that which exists in acute hospitals) and move into a psychosocial model of care, and (3) elevate patient rights. These regulations met with much resistance from the nursing home industry, which claimed that the switch of emphasis would be too costly. As a result, nothing significant happened until 1987.

As we have seen in the preceding sections of this chapter, both the public and the country's leaders realized that there is a real need for nursing home care reform. Nonetheless, it still took a very long time before the federal government issued its regulations governing the operations of nursing homes facilities.

This finally happened in 1987, when Congress and the Health Care Facilities Association (HCFA) enacted the most comprehensive overhaul of the nursing facilities and federal government's regulation since the enactment of the Medicare and Medicaid programs in the mid-1960's. This new law is called the Omnibus Budget Reconciliation Act 1987 (OBRA). The law stipulates that nursing homes are to be considered homes for the people who live in these facilities, and those who reside in them should be considered residents and not patients. At the same time, nursing homes are also truly convalescent hospitals or skilled nursing facilities for those patients on short stay, paid by Medicare and private insurance. Under these new regulations, uniform standards of staffing adequacy and quality of care are to be enforced nationwide. Some of the states initially boycotted the idea of federal control. However, after giving the states a few years to reconsider their position, the federal government informed the states that if they did not wish to comply, the federal government would send their own inspectors in to do the inspection work, and the state would receive no Medicare/Medicaid payments. The strength in this legislation is that all states must comply with these regulations and guidelines or forfeit the substantial federal funding. The federal government could even follow-up on state inspectors with an inspection of their own on the same facility to verify if indeed the federal guidelines had been satisfied. The late Senator Heinz had wanted to create a strong, effective enforcement system for all inspectors at the state level to follow. Perhaps, more importantly, he had wanted to ensure that if the established level of care is not met, appropriate and swift penalties would be dealt out.[14] Since 1991 all states have adjusted their local regulations to conform to the federal regulations and guidelines. In 1993, there was even a new infusion of financial support in the form of increased Medicaid payments for nursing home care.

Having a set of well-defined guidelines is one thing. Effective enforcement of the provisions of the guidelines is often another matter. Even though federal and state governments began to implement the OBRA guidelines in 1987, the problem of uniform quality of care takes much longer to resolve, and it still exists today in nursing homes nationwide. A HCFA report released in December 1988 says 25 percent of nursing homes nationwide failed to give drugs according to physician's order, and 45 percent did not prepare or serve food under sanitary conditions.[15]

There are several positive notes to add. Contemporary nursing homes are entering into a new era. Most of these facilities are providing a distinct Medicare unit or a sub-acute unit for residents who are truly there for rehabilitation purposes. These units deliver more intensive medical care

---

[14]See footnote 7.
[15]U.S. Senate Committee on Aging, 101st Congress. Federal Implementation of OBRA 1987 Nursing Home Reform Provisions. May 18, 1989, p.39.

and skilled nursing care services (tracheotomy care and suctioning, ventilator management, and intravenous fluid therapy programs) plus extensive rehabilitation services (physical therapy, occupational therapy, speech therapy and medical social worker), for both the elderly as well as the not-so-old residents. Some of the facilities are also providing a special care unit for Alzheimer residents. They are in the process of admitting terminally ill AIDS residents, as well as hospice residents with terminal cancer diagnoses. In these units, highly trained as well as certified nursing assistants are all specialists in their own field with many years of experience. The presence of these highly skilled and trained personnel in a facility often leads to enhanced professionalism, which filters down into the remaining parts of the long-term care units. Furthermore, most of the facilities are trying to reduce the dependence of their residents on chemical and physical restraints (to be discussed in later chapters); the concept of an interdisciplinary care team poised to provide not only medical but psychosocial assessment and care is beginning to become a reality (see below).

The OBRA Guidelines for Resident Assessment[16]

Every facility that wishes to participate in the federal Medicare and Medicaid programs must assess each resident using the **Resident Assessment Instrument (RAI)**. There are four components to this instrument:

1. **Minimum Data Set (MDS)**
2. **Resident Assessment Protocol Worksheet (Triggers)**
3. **Resident Assessment Protocol Summary (RAPS)**
4. **Care Plan and Nurse's Summary Sheet.**

---

[16]U.S. Senate Committee on Aging, 101st Congress, Workshop on Resident Assessment: The Springboard to Quality of Care and Quality of Life for Nursing Home Residents, Serial No. 101-30, U.S. Government Printing Office, 1991, pp.85

Assuming that your loved one has decided to enter a convalescent hospital, a comprehensive assessment and screening of him/her will be made in accordance with the resident assessment instrument. This instrument in its entirety constitutes a dramatic overhaul of the manner that nursing homes care for their residents. Both you and your loved one as client/resident will have significant input in all the subject areas that are being assessed. Your input will give you and your loved one the ammunition to demand self-autonomy, self-control over his/her own life, self-dignity and respect. The RAI covers those broad aspects of one's life, ranging from cognitive abilities of the individual such as seeing, listening, reasoning and communicating, to more physical and medical problems such as physiological functioning and skin condition. The individual's nutritional status, his/her psychosocial makeup and his/her activity pattern are also evaluated.

The first step of the assessment is to complete the **Minimum Data Set (MDS).** This provides basic screening and assessment items to identify each individual resident's strengths, weaknesses, preferences, needs, and contributing factors to problems. Implementing this complex and multifaceted tool requires an interdisciplinary team approach. The RN is assigned as the case coordinator for the completion of the MDS. All other health professionals must assess and complete their designated sections. This whole assessment process requires gathering information from the resident, past medical records, staff members, family members, the primary care physician, physical therapist, occupational therapist, speech therapist, medical social worker and rehabilitation aide. The reason for this comprehensive evaluation process is that the consensus among healthcare professionals points to the fact that the evaluation of the elderly requires a different approach from that used for younger individuals. They agree that a medical diagnosis used alone has many limitations for those suffering from chronic illness. Since an individual's physical, mental, and social well-being are closely interrelated, an assessment needs to consider all these factors in combination. The emphasis of the MDS is on the level of functioning rather than on the presence or absence of a disease. It takes into account the individual holistically. An accurate and comprehensive MDS requires at least 2 to 3 hours to complete depending on the complexities of the individual resident's conditions. Federal regulation requires each individual staff who completes a portion of the assessment to sign and verify its accuracy. This gives you as the consumer a powerful tool because you may query any person on the team as to where she obtained the information entered into the record and on its accuracy. In each of those areas checked for possible intervention, one or more of the eighteen "triggers" are alerted. These trigger items relate to areas in need of more in-depth assessment.

The second step is the **Resident Assessment Protocol Worksheet (Triggers)**. All identified problems will be given either a dot (for automatic activation) or a triangle (for potential activation) with a number (1-18) attached to it. Any potential triggers must be documented in the nurse's progress summary sheet with a reason why it will not be acted upon at this time. Activation means that the triggered item is now subject to the Resident Assessment Protocol (RAP) guidelines. In this trigger phase, the team must go back to the MDS looking for the nature of the problems, causing them to identify things that may have contributed to the problem in the first place. This process encourages the staff to focus on how a resident's strengths, weaknesses, preferences, and needs in one area will affect those in another area. It is an organizational tool suggesting that the individual resident either has a current problem, a chronic problem, an inactive problem, or is at high risk of developing a new problem if given no preventative or rehabilitative intervention. The team must factually document why any new health problems were clinically unavoidable. The team must also conscientiously try to limit the use of chemical and physical restraints to subdue residents. In this manner, each resident in the facility becomes a person, not just a room and bed number. With this type of holistic approach, the goals are to maximize individual resident's independent functions and to improve the quality of life and care for each resident.

The third step is the **Resident Assessment Protocol Summary (RAPS)**. This summary provides an important link between MDS assessment and the development of an individualized care plan. There are 18 conditions that lead to automatic triggering of a more in-depth assessment. When these triggered problems are further assessed, and it is concluded that certain specific problems still exist under this scrutiny, then they must be entered into the Care Plan in 7 days some of the other problems are monitored for 14 days and modified within 21 days after admission. If there is any significant change of condition, a new MDS must be completely done, and a new care plan drawn up. This makes the staff assess each new and old admission very carefully, because no one wants to redo the whole process again. Typically about 4 to 8 RAP conditions are triggered for each resident. This process eliminates a laundry list of problems and duplications. It makes the care plan a useful and essential tool for the caring of that individual resident.

The automatically triggered RAP list includes:
1. Delirium - Does the resident suffer from an acute short-term confused or disoriented state which may be reversible if detected and treated in a timely fashion? Are there any indications of confusion and disorientation in thinking awareness? Is he/she less alert, less aware of the environment? Has he/she had periods of incoherent speech, motor restlessness or lethargy, and does his/her mental clarity vary during the course of the day? Has there been any change of these conditions within the last three months? What is the presumed cause of the resident's change in

mental status or behavior that deviates from his/her usual state? Could the change be drug related?

2. Cognitive loss/Dementia (mental status) - This assessment includes testing for long and short-term memory problems and recall ability. It assesses the ability of an individual to make decisions regarding tasks of daily living. However, in this case, the effects may or may not be reversible. As one can see, #1 and #2 are closely interrelated. Dementia can be a medical diagnosis or drug-related. Have there been any changes during the last three months?

3. Communication/hearing patterns - The intent here is to define a resident's ability to hear, to understand and to communicate with others with assistive hearing devices. The ability of the resident to express or to communicate requests, needs, opinions, urgent problems, and social conversation is evaluated. Can he/she comprehend the verbal information? This is assessed in the first 7 days. Have there been any changes within the last three months?

4. Vision patterns - This is the ability of the resident to see close objects in adequate lighting such as reading a newspaper without difficulty. Are there any visual limitations due to cataracts, glaucoma, macular degeneration, diabetic retinopathy or other diseases? Does the resident use any visual appliances such as glasses, a magnifying glass or contact lenses?

5. ADL/Physical function and rehabilitation potential - In this area of evaluation, the licensed staff and the Certified Nursing Assistants (CNA) will determine the resident's level of self-care performance in activities of daily living (ADL). How much assistance do staff members need to provide in activities such as bed mobility, transfer, locomotion, dressing, eating, toilet use, personal hygiene, bathing, and body control problems due to contractures of arms shoulders, legs, or hands? Is there partial or total loss of voluntary leg or arm movement (paralysis)? Does he/she need mobility appliances? Can the resident do his/her ADL partially if the duties are divided into sections? Most of the residents have some deficits with memory, with the thinking process or with simply paying attention to the task due to problems such as dementia, CVA (stroke), or depression. Is there any functional/rehabilitation potential in ADL? In other words, is there any chance for the resident to become independent if there are rehabilitative and restorative programs such as feeding retraining, grooming, dressing or toileting? These are also assessed in the first 7 days. Are there any changes over the last three months?

6. Incontinence of urine and bowel - Is there a history of urinary tract infections or episodes of fecal impaction? Does the resident use laxatives routinely? Does the resident use any appliances such as an external catheter or diaper? Is he/she on any program such as a toileting plan or a bowel/bladder retraining program? Have there been any changes in the last three months? Most of the patients transferred from an acute care hospital will come with a foley catheter which was inserted on the day they were admitted to that hospital. Depending on the duration that the catheter has been in the bladder, the bladder will generally need retraining. Otherwise, there is a chance that the person will not be able to void without assistance. If he/she is incontinent, what is the culprit? Can it be resolved or eliminated? Should the bowel and bladder retraining programs be initiated? These will be observed for 14 days.

7. Psychosocial well-being - Is the resident able to participate in various activities? Is he/she happy or unhappy with his/her roommate or other residents? Can he/she openly express conflict/anger/joy with family members or friends? The team will evaluate the ability of the resident to adjust to his/her new environment taking into consideration his/her past experience and professional stature. Since it usually takes an individual approximately 21 days to adjust to any new changes, this part of the assessment is completed within that 21 day period.

8. Mood patterns - Is the resident able to verbalize about anxiety, grief or hopelessness? Does he/she exhibit tearfulness, groaning, sighing, pacing, hand wringing, or have recurrent thoughts of death or suicide? Does this mood appear daily or infrequently? Have there been any changes in the last 90 days?

9. Behavior problems - Are there any behavior problems? Is the resident verbally or physically abusive? Does he/she exhibit socially inappropriate and disruptive behavior? Does he/she wander? Have any of these problems changed during the past 90 days? Points #8 and #9 are related, and they belong to the domain of the Social Service Department.

10. Activity pursuit patterns - How often is the resident awake? What is the average daily time that the resident is involved in activities? What types of activities does he/she enjoy? Does he/she request other choice of activities? Does he/she like to go on outings? Points #7, #8, #9 and #10 are very closely interrelated. This is where the Activity Director can provide the most input.

11. Falls - The team will identify specific problems or symptoms that could affect the resident's health or functional status with respect to balance and coordination. Risk factors for functional decline such as dizziness/vertigo, edema, internal bleeding, hallucinations/delusions (the resident behaves as if he/she sees, hears, smells, or tastes things others do not, has false ideas not shared by others, talks to self or to a deceased person, hears voices) and/or fainting spells are identified. Have there been any falls within the last 30, 90, and 180 days?

12. Nutritional status - Are there any chewing, swallowing or mouth problems or pain? What is the resident's current height and weight? How is his/her appetite? Does he/she refuse his/her meals? Is he/she malnourished? The dietitian makes these assessments with inputs from the Nursing Department.

13. Feeding tube - Does the resident have a tube that delivers nutritional substances directly into the stomach? Was a speech therapist involved in evaluating a swallowing problem? Has oral feeding been attempted? When was the last attempt? Both the nursing department and the dietary department are involved in this assessment.

14. Dehydration/fluid maintenance - What is the resident's intake and output in a 24-hour period? Are there any problems with elimination via bowel or bladder? Was there any acute episode of fecal impaction? The CNA input is important here.

15. Dental care - Does the resident have any dentures, bridges or other dental appliances? Does the resident wear them? Are there any problems associated with the dentures? Are they broken or loose? Does he/she have carious teeth? Is there any debris in the mouth? Does he/she have established daily routines for the cleaning of his/her mouth, teeth or dentures? The resident, his/her family members will coordinate inputs with the nursing, dietary and social service departments.

16. Pressure sores (bedsores, decubitus) - Are there any stasis ulcers or pressure sores? How severe are the pressure sores if they do exist? Are any special devices, treatments, and procedures prescribed for the existing condition? Older residents with poor circulation and those who spend much time in bed are prone to developing these pressure sores. Assessing these requires skilled nursing judgment.

17. Psychotropic drug use (chemical restraints) - Does the resident take any prescribed antipsychotic, antidepressant, antianxiety, or hypnotic drugs? How often are they taken? Has there been a recent assessment of the effectiveness of those drugs in controlling the specific mood or behavior problem by the physician or the pharmacy consultant? Why is he/she using these drugs? Have there been any attempts to taper off the usage of these drugs? Have any alternative methods of treatment been tried before? The input from family members is very important in this area.

18. Physical restraints - During the last seven days, has the resident used any type of equipment such as bed rails, trunk/limb restraints or a chair that prevents him/her from rising? What are the reasons for the use of these special devices? Have there been any attempts to eliminate these devices? Are alternative methods being attempted? Again, your input as the responsible family member is essential here.

The fourth and last step is the most crucial step because it involves the actual development of an individualized **Care Plan.** During this step the interdisciplinary team members evaluate and discuss the problems that are identified in the RAPS and formulate a care plan. It is important that the care plan includes the resident's own reasonable and reachable goals set by him/herself, a time limit to reach them and his/her approaches to achieve these goals. With the help and guidance of the interdisciplinary team, an appropriate rehabilitation therapy program that is tailored to his/her special needs can be developed. This care plan is then transmitted to all staff members for usage in the care of that individual resident.

Considered altogether, these four steps provide specific information and methods of care for each resident. Each is assessed from a psychosocial perspective as well as a medical perspective. Inputs from the resident and his/her family are crucial on all of these items. Accurate and factual information are very important to the interdisciplinary team, who will write the summary note on why some of the triggered problems will not commence with treatment at this time. After admission, this process of review by the interdisciplinary team is done four times a year, and the complete MDS is reviewed and updated yearly.

As you can see by the above protocol, the goals and objectives of the facility and the inspectors are: to focus on quality facility performance and resident's outcome rather than on procedural or paperwork requirements; to require that all facilities provide each resident with the necessary individualized medical, nursing, and psychosocial services; and to rehabilitate the individual resident either fully or partially in his/her activities of daily living so that he/she can go home, enter a residential care facility, a retirement facility, or a board-and-care facility. OBRA also requires standardized training of facility personnel and inspectors alike on the regulations and interpretive guidelines of the law. In this manner, the facility staff and the inspectors will have a common goal: to attain or to maintain each resident at the highest physical, mental and psychosocial well-being possible and to achieve the highest quality of life and quality of care for all residents. The physical appearance of the facility and paper work documentation are secondary in importance.

During their annual visit, the inspectors are looking at problems and approaches identified on the care plan to verify that they are being carried out on the floor by all the staff. They can pick a staff member randomly to question her about those residents she is taking care of. They will find out if she knows the problems of this individual, and whether she is following the care plan. They can also choose to interview any residents regarding the care given to them by the staff. Inspectors can even attend resident council meetings. This time under OBRA, all state inspectors are given mandated control over Medicare and Medicaid reimbursement. All deficiencies become Class-A (very serious) citations no matter how minor or how life-threatening. Finally, the inspectors are truly representing the resident's welfare.

Sometimes the inspecting team can go from a partial inspection to a full blown inspection, putting the facility on "fast track" or even taking over the facility for a short duration in order to elicit rapid improvement in the quality of care for the residents. Hopefully by taking these steps a strong message is sent to the nursing home providers that the public will not tolerate substandard care anymore. The next few chapters will examine in detail many of the areas in which the public can help the inspectors bring about major beneficial changes for the residents in these nursing homes.

CHAPTER 3

Nursing Home Types, Ownership, Organization

Types of Facilities..31
Ownership/Proprietorship...35
Facility Staff...40

We have seen in the last chapter that nursing homes have indeed undergone major changes over the years. With the federal OBRA regulations in place and the RAI instrument as the approach to resident care within these facilities, we are comforted that there is some standardization upon which we can judge a facility. The next thing that the consumer needs in order to make intelligent decisions in the placement of a loved one is the knowledge of facilities available to him. If you look into the Yellow Pages of the telephone book you will see a large number of skilled nursing facilities listed. How do you know where to start? In order to narrow the options, you need to know something about the makeup of these facilities. First, the different types of facilities will be discussed. Secondly, because the type of ownership of a facility could influence the manner that care is given to the residents, a discussion of the several types of ownership and their special features will be made. Finally, each facility has its staff for the care of the residents and the maintenance of the facility. A list of several individuals that you would meet upon entering a convalescent hospital will be given.

Types of Facilities

NURSING HOMES/CONVALESCENT HOSPITALS /SKILLED NURSING FACILITIES:

There are several types of facilities that take care of senior citizens, but only one type of long-term care facility will take care of the chronically ill or the disabled elderly with major mental and physical impairments. Such a facility is often called a nursing home, a convalescent hospital or a skilled nursing facility interchangeably by consumers and professionals alike. Actually, the long-term care facility usually constitutes the main part of the convalescent hospital. The size of the skilled nursing component of a facility varies. Irrespective of the name, regulations that govern the operations of all of these facilities are the same.

The **long-term care** part of the nursing home is required by law to have Licensed Vocational Nurses (LVNs) on duty twenty-four hours a day, seven days per week. If the facility has less than 60 beds, only one RN Supervisor/ Director of Nurses is needed. If the facility has as many as ninety-nine beds, then there will be a Registered Nurse (RN) on duty eight hours a day on the day shift, seven days per week. For facilities with one hundred beds and up, an RN must be on duty twenty-four hours a day, seven days per week. Physicians must visit each of the residents at least once a month. The vast majority of these long-term residents needing custodial care are widowed women who are poor and have no close family ties. Some suffer from a large number of emotional, mental, and physical disabilities. Some are incontinent of both bowel and bladder functions. Some need assistance in all aspects of activities of daily living (ADL). Some are totally confused and disoriented and no longer able to live outside. Some simply have no other place to live.[17] They will reside in the nursing home for many years, often until they die. The facility's goals for these residents focus on restoration, maintaining or slowing of the loss of functioning, and alleviation of discomfort/pain.

---

[17]Committee on Nursing Home Regulation, Institute of Medicine, Improving the Quality of Care in Nursing Homes, National Academy Press, Washington, D.C., 1986, pp 5-6.

Ideally, achieving these goals will make these later years of life more vigorous, healthy, and satisfying instead of merely adding years. The Certified Nursing Assistants (CNAs are the front-line nursing personnel for achieving these goals. The facility must also provide a comprehensive range of services to be specifically developed and coordinated to meet the medical, nursing, physical, emotional and psycho-social needs of the chronically ill and disabled geriatric residents. They must provide a protective environment for the residents who cannot take care of themselves outside anymore. This is where the rehabilitation aide's services are used. She is under the direction supervision of the physical therapist.

Actual **skilled nursing services** consist of only a small, distinct part of the main convalescent hospital. The residents of this extended care group (skilled nursing patients), come from the acute hospital after an illness or an injury. They are in the transition stage, still too weak and sick to go home, but not sick enough to be in the acute care hospital. They may be young, middle aged or elderly, but they are all alert, oriented and their stay is short term. The aim and the goal for this group of residents is to return the individual to his/her previous level of independence, either partially or totally. This part operates under the guidelines of Medicare Part A, the federal government's hospital insurance program for the patients who qualify for the care. The guidelines and criteria for such operation will be discussed in a later chapter titled "Medicare". The physician visits these patients/residents in this component of the nursing home more often than they do for the long-term care residents. Within this component, there must be a registered nurse (RN) on duty twenty-four hours a day, seven days per week. These CNAs must have had at least two years of geriatric experience in a nursing home setting. There must be an active rehabilitation program with daily or at least five days per week schedule. All of these services are under the direct supervision of the physicians.

Thus a nursing home is considered a home for some and a convalescent/skilled nursing facility for others. Life in such a facility involves both medical care and social service supports. For most of the residents nursing homes represent physical, emotional, psychosocial, spiritual, and environmental security.

INTERMEDIATE CARE FACILITIES :

The residents living in these facilities are relatively independent and require only minimum care. They are usually able to control their bowel and bladder functions; they use either a cane walker or a wheelchair for mobility. Most of these residents are not capable of completely independent living but just require assistance with their ADL care. These facilities provide minimal medical, nursing and social services. They also must comply with federal and state regulations, but the regulations are not as stringent as those for the skilled nursing facilities. There are very few of these facilities today.

RESIDENTIAL CARE FACILITIES:

These privately owned places provide a safe, hygienic and sheltered living arrangement for people fully capable of functional independence. These facilities stress residents' social needs. They do not generally provide any medical or nursing services. Room, board, and some laundry and housekeeping services are provided. There are no established government regulations as stringent as those governing either the skilled nursing facilities or the intermediate care facilities. These facilities vary in size, ownership, classification, type, resident population, structured services and source of payment. Most of the space (apartments) in these facilities will be reserved for private-pay senior citizens. The management of these facilities usually reserve a small percentage of the apartments for those on governmental assistance.

Some of these residential facilities have a "step-up" program. Besides the totally independent living arrangement, there is a class called the "Personal Care" living arrangement. At this level, the facility's staff will provide assistance with daily care and remind the resident to take his/her medication. He/she must go to the common dining room for his/her meals. An even higher level of care that is offered by some of these facilities is called "Private Nursing Care". This is a service that is provided to a resident who is totally unable to do anything for him/herself anymore, but still resides in the residential facility. Basically, it is like having a nursing home's services brought to your own apartment. The resident will be responsible for all expenses of the nursing services rendered. Not many people can afford this type of care for very long before they exhaust all their savings and assets. For this component, the facility would have to comply with all the regulations just like any other nursing facility.

Nursing homes that operate to receive federal reimbursement must be licensed by the state for both Medicare and Medicaid programs. An overwhelming majority of the nursing homes operate in that manner. There are, however, some exceptions. These few facilities are strictly private nursing facilities in that they accept only private-pay residents. They need not to have applied for Medicare or Medicaid licensing. It may be argued that these facilities might turn out to be the unregulated, subpar facilities, but often the market-place incentive forces these facilities to maintain a high level of care and responsibility.

Ownership/Proprietorship:

In the last chapter an overview on how the nursing home industry came into existence was presented. In this section, the different types of nursing home ownership will be outlined. There are at least five types of proprietorships. First, some nursing homes are owned and managed by large corporations. Second, there are individually or family run operations. Third, a new trend now is for acute hospitals to manage a subsidiary nursing home and consider it as a "step-down" unit of the hospital. Fourth, some of the retirement villages or residential care facilities own and manage a nursing home as an option for a "step up" level of care. Finally, there are a few facilities that are operated by churches or other non-profit or not-for-profit organizations. Since the "step-down" or "step-up" manifestations can be found in any of the other three proprietary groupings, categorizing of these facilities will be done by proprietary grouping alone, of which there are just three: corporation run, privately run, and non-profit run. Since the passage of the federal OBRA regulations, irrespective of the type of ownership, each facility has to meet the same stringent regulations. This uniform set of guidelines and interpretations must be applied by all inspectors and facilities in the entire United States.

The corporate managed nursing home usually is a chain facility belonging to a large "health care" or service-directed corporation. As with all corporations, all decisions of the corporation are made by the Board of Directors (BOD) and the stockholders. Often, the delivery of quality care to residents will take a backseat to more pressing issues such as acquisitions, mergers, and devising schemes to keep regulators off their back. Enlightened BODs do indeed exist, and the best or the worst of corporate run facilities depend greatly on these members.

If a nursing home is part of a chain that is owned and operated by a nationwide corporation, then each of the units must operate under corporate policies as well as state and federal government regulations. The larger the corporation, the more resources and bureaucracy they have. These corporations have their own internal quality assurance team whose job is to routinely visit different facilities under their charge to monitor various departments for the quality of life and care for all their residents. With respect to assessing quality assurance in nursing departments, corporate-run nursing homes utilize RNs who have had acute-care experience as well as skilled nursing home experience. These nurses hold the titles such as Professional Services Consultant (PSC). They will visit the facilities under their charge, making quality assurance rounds and monitoring all aspects of the care. They also serve as resource personnel for the individual facility's Director of Nursing. They provide emotional support and in-service education for the nursing staff. The corporate pharmacy consultant will monitor all the medication regimen. Other departments are also audited by appropriate consultants during these visits. These consultants will grade each facility on its level of care. If they find that a particular facility is not meeting the corporation standards, they will notify the corporation's Director of Nurses, who in turn will contact a Professional Service Specialist(PSS). The PSS enters the flagged facility as a teacher and a specialist to help that facility set up approaches to eliminate the immediate problems.

Two advantages of corporate operated nursing homes are uniformity in striving for quality and adequacy in the number of staff. Often corporate regulations are stricter than state mandates, thus placing higher quality of care as a corporate goal. These facilities usually also maintain adequate staffing and sufficient supplies to accommodate all the residents' needs. In addition, the local administration benefits from receiving up-to-date informational materials which help the staff keep abreast with the continuing changes in regulations coming from both the corporation and the governmental agencies.

In order to maintain the same level of care as a large, well-funded corporate facility, most of the smaller **private individually and family owned** facilities have to resort to hiring an outside Consultant under contract, to periodically conduct the type of quality assurances described above. Because the contractual obligations of consultants are not standardized, and the reporting authority differs from one facility to the next, these consultants operate with differences in goals. Often they provide more destructive criticisms than they give positive reinforcements. When I was a Director of Nursing in one of these facilities, I was lucky to have had a consultant who acted as my springboard for new ideas. She listened to my frustrations and gave me suggestions. She gave in-service classes to my nursing staff whenever I requested them during her monthly visit.

Since the conditions of some of the residents within a facility can change frequently, solely relying on the external consultant for quality assurance and evaluation is always inadequate. The Medical Records clerk and the Director of Nursing need to perform their own audits of the facility on a weekly basis. Unfortunately, two things conspire to make this arrangement hard to fulfill. First of all, the communication between the DON and the Medical Records clerk often breaks down for political "turf" reasons, and one blames the other. Secondly, as is the case with many small business enterprises, often they are struggling to stay solvent, and the proprietor will cut corners to keep the business afloat. Most of the time, the owner and the administration of a small facility and the nursing department do not see eye to eye because of a difference in philosophy. The former is geared toward financial solvency while the latter wants to focus on the residents' welfare. When an administration's concern is not resident-oriented, that attitude permeates to the residents through the enforced attitudes of the department heads, which in turn are reflected in the morale of the staff. On the other hand, if the administrator and the owner treat the staff with respect and dignity, supporting the staff's efforts, then the residents will also benefit. Unfortunately, there just are not many enlightened owners.

One facility where I had worked before did have a different outlook. This was a family owned facility where staffing was largely filled by the dedicated members of a church-affiliated group of health professionals. The owner's family members, all of whom were nurses or managers, and other church members who were nurses or certified nursing assistants, occupied most of the staff positions. We all had genuine concern for residents' welfare at heart. The owner also helped with individual staff's personal problems. We treated all the staff with respect and dignity, each person being treated like a valued family member. On special occasions all staff received gifts. There were holiday banquets that were cooked by the owner's family, and the entire staff and their families were invited. The morale and team spirit of the staff were very high. As a result, the staff's performance level was correspondingly high, to the benefit of the residents. There was always a waiting list for prospective residents to come in, and the staff turn-over was almost nil. All staff received merit increases routinely. This facility was reported in the local newspaper as being one of the best in the Sacramento area at that time.

The non-profit or not-for-profit facilities are not owned by shareholders. They are established for altruistic purposes as a component of a non-profit organization's attempt to fulfill a need in the community. Churches and community action groups are the most common organizations that can muster the resources to operate a nursing home. They do, however, have their own Board of Directors and can accept donations, raise funds and purchase goods with tax-exempt status. The Directors are community-based citizens with various educational and professional backgrounds. They set policies based on the federal and state regulations. In these facilities, the Board of Directors hires an Administrator. The Administrator in turn hires the Director of Nursing with a contracted Nurse Consultant's approval. The day-to-day functions of the nursing home are left to the facility personnel. The Nurse Consultant comes to the facility once a month to do an evaluation of the nursing department and gives a written report to the Administrator and the Director of Nursing on any deficiencies. It is then up to the Nursing Department personnel to correct them before the next visit. There is also a contracted pharmacy consultant who reviews all residents' drug regimens. Each facility has its own Medical Record Department, and one of its functions is to conduct internal audits. For these facilities, the Board of Directors usually meets once a month. The Administrator reports all the operations to them and then brings back policies the Board wants the facility to adopt. If the Administrator supports the Director of Nursing, and if there is an open line of communication between those two offices, then the facility will operate with a unified goal from the top. The interaction between the contracted Nurse Consultant and the Director of Nursing is equally vital. It is necessary that the Nurse Consultant serves both as the quality assurance officer and the support and nurturing agent. In this manner, the non-profit facilities and those of small, private ownership facilities are alike in the need to establish and maintain communication regarding resident care and staff welfare.

Facility staff[18]

Every facility has the following staff personnel. Most of these people are on duty five days per week on the day shift. Several categories of nursing home personnel must be on duty throughout the 24-hour periods. These will be noted. When you have any problems and complaints be sure to talk with one of them.

1. ADMINISTRATOR

He/she is responsible for the organization and management of the facility. He/she is responsible for managing the budget and ensuring financial stability, enforcing federal, state, local regulations, hiring, terminating, supervising department heads, and

---

[18]Richards, Marty et al., Choosing a Nursing Home: A Guidebook for Families, Modified and reprinted with permission from U. of Washington Press, Seattle, 1985, pp 85-94.

representing the facility in the community. The "buck" stops with him/her.

2. DIRECTOR OF NURSING

She has the overall responsibility for patient care delivered in a nursing home. She ensures that nursing services are carried out with safety, efficiency, and regard for the resident's privacy and dignity. She plays a primary role in selecting patients for admission. She hires, terminates, and supervises all personnel in the nursing department. Since nursing is the largest department in the nursing home, she also has extensive authority to coordinate all services over other departments.

3. PHYSICIAN

Every resident must have a physician's order to be admitted to a facility. The physician must visit the new resident within seventy-two hours after admission. After that the physician is required to visit the resident at least once a month. Every physician must have an alternate physician. Each facility must have a Medical Director. This individual oversees all functions, responsibilities and duties of the professional medical staff.

4. REGISTERED NURSE

She holds the supervisory position in the nursing home. She is the person who will call the physician whenever there is a change of condition in the resident's health status and is directly responsible for resolving resident's needs. Depending on the size of the facility, RNs may be on duty at all times. Go to her if you have any complaints on direct resident care.

5. LICENSED VOCATIONAL NURSES

They are the charge nurses of the units. They pass medications, perform treatments and write weekly summaries. They should be able to answer all the concerns of your loved one. They are always on duty 24-hours a day, seven days per week.

6. CERTIFIED NURSING ASSISTANTS

These are the front-line nurses who attend to the resident's daily care. The resident's well-being (or non-well-being) are totally dependent on them. They are the eyes, ears, nose and touch of the licensed nurses. When they report any change of condition of a particular resident to the nurses early, then intervention starts early, and the resident's suffering is minimized. They are the most important team members of the nursing department. There will be CNAs on duty 24-hours a day, seven days per week.

7. DIRECTOR OF STAFF DEVELOPMENT

She is the individual who has the responsibility to keep the skill level of the staff up to par. Her primary responsibility is that of an educator. She has the orientation duties for all new, incoming employees. She teaches in-service classes for all staff, particularly the nursing staff who need annual in-service hours. She is also responsible for training new nursing assistants and certifying them to become CNAs. Sometimes she also functions as the infection control nurse.

8. OFFICE MANAGER

She is the business manager of the facility. She interacts with the residents and families immediately upon their entering the facility. She maintains their individual accounts, and keeps track of their expenses and personal items. She is also responsible for settling accounts with Medicare and Medicaid personnel.

9. MEDICAL RECORD CLERK

She sets up the new admission medical record for the nursing department and all other departments to complete. She manages all the resident's clinical medical records, both current and past. She continuously audits medical records entries to ensure that all department personnel comply with the regulations.

10. ACTIVITIES DIRECTOR

She develops, schedules, and conducts a multifaceted program geared to meet the social, recreational, and diversional needs of all residents. She is the person who is responsible for buying cigarettes for residents.

11. SOCIAL SERVICE DIRECTOR

She is usually the one to interact with the family members on non-medical and psychosocial issues. These include roommate problems, smoking problems, and the need to establish transportation for outpatient visits.

12. DIETARY SUPERVISOR

She works closely with the registered dietitian consultant and the nursing department to ensure that the meals taste good, look attractive and are nutritionally well-balanced. She supervises her staff who include several cooks and nutritional assistants. Make sure that you work very closely with her if you find that your loved one does not like some of the foods on the meal tray. She can do some substitution as long as the request is not too extravagant.

13. LAUNDRY SUPERVISOR

She supervises her staff in washing all residents' bed linens and their personal clothes daily. She also orders all new linens, bedspreads and underpads. She ensures that when her staff transports clean linen from the laundry to the floor, the carts are covered. When picking up soiled linen from the floor, she ensures that the storage bin cover is covered tightly to prevent the spread of infection.

14. HOUSEKEEPING/MAINTENANCE SUPERVISOR

Sometimes the facility combines these two departments under one supervisor. They maintain a safe, clean, secure environment. The maintenance Supervisor monitors the whole building structure inside and out. Anything that pertains to electrical equipment must be approved by him. Housekeepers do the light activities such as cleaning of bathrooms and mopping of bathroom, bedroom floors and hallways. The janitors do the heavy-duty work such as cleaning and waxing the floors for the whole facility.

Now that you have some information on the types of nursing homes and residential facilities, and some idea how ownership style may affect the services delivered, you will be able to carefully weigh those considerations when you choose a nursing home to fit you and your loved one's needs. That is the subject of the next chapter.

CHAPTER 4

Choosing a Nursing Home

Points to Consider in Choosing a Nursing Home................47
    External Factors...47
    Internal Environment......................................48
The Tell-Tale Signs...50
Staffing Adequacy...53

In the last two chapters, we have seen that the nursing home industry developed in what amounts to an unregulated manner until very recently. As a result, there is much non-uniformity both in the manner of nursing home operation as well as in the delivery of needed care. As a potential clientele of this industry, it is necessary for you to take note of these variables. Some of the significant variables could very well affect the quality of care given to your loved one, once he/she is placed in a nursing home. One of the variables is the manner of management and ownership of the facility. This topic was discussed in the previous chapter. The objective of this chapter is to provide you with objective criteria upon which you can evaluate and choose the facility most suited to the needs of your loved one. You will also have to take into consideration a third variable, that is of how your own financial situation can affect the range of your choices. A separate chapter will be devoted to details of financing stays in the nursing home.

The cost of a nursing home stay for those residents who have adequate means as a private-paying patient is between three to five thousand dollars a month. For those who are on limited Medicare coverage, or have private insurance coverage, the options for a short stay in a skilled nursing facility are quite numerous. You, as the responsible party for your loved one, should take the process of deciding which facility is the right one very seriously. You have the upper hand. Most of the facilities will be trying to impress you with their apparent concern for your loved one. Do not let the high-pressure sales mannerism of a particular facility push you into a decision before you are ready to commit.

If your loved one has inadequate financial resources the choices of placement will be somewhat limited. That is because Medicaid reimbursement to the facility is often just a small percentage of what the facility can charge the private-pay resident. For this reason, that individual would have a very difficult time finding a facility that is willing to take him/her. Money aside, there are several other reasons for such a situation. Number one on the list is that it is hard to find a private physician who is willing to accept the responsibility of care for your loved one in a particular nursing home if your loved one's own physician refuses to come to that facility. The second reason is most of the designated Medicaid beds are usually already occupied by the truly long-term, custodial care residents. The third reason is that your loved one may be put on a "Medicaid pending" status by the state. As a result, the facility may not want to "take the chance" of your loved one's Medicaid insurance falling through and not be able to collect. In this case you can go to the State Department of Social Welfare and push them to speed up the process. You can also seek the help of the State's Ombudsman.

When you decide to visit convalescent hospitals, you need to have in your possession a list of potential candidate facilities. You might have already obtained the names of several of these facilities from the hospital's patient care coordinator, or you may have gotten them from the telephone book. After initial screening for the convenience of their locations to you or your own neighborhood, you will need to formulate a visitation plan. Your first impression and knowing exactly what you are looking for are very important to your final decision. If time permits, do not limit your search and do not lower your expectations. You should know what to expect in a nursing home, but you need also to remember that a nursing home becomes a home to most of the residents and not just a hospital. Above all, you should expect good care from those staff members in the areas of their expertise. If your loved one is coming to the nursing home directly from home, try to bring him/her with you to visit the facility before the final decision is made.

Points to consider in choosing the right skilled nursing home/convalescent hospital:

I External Factors
A. The convenience and location of the facility
　　Since a convalescent hospital is intended to be used for long term residents as well as for sub-acutely ill patients in short-term stays, daily visits over a long period of time dictate that convenient location be a factor to be considered. You need to envision what the trek will be like a few weeks or months after the initial placement. You do not want this aspect be a "drag" on your relationship with your loved one. For your loved one to have that continuing contact with you will decrease or totally eliminate the fears that you both have about such a stay. Visitations from the home front may even speed up the rehabilitation period. Things to consider are:
　　1. How far is the facility to your home, to other family members' homes? Is there public transportation and how far is the bus stop from the facility? Is the location safe when walking alone after it gets dark? Safety is very important for you and your loved one's peace of mind.
　　2. How far is the facility to the necessary medical offices of your loved one? This includes the nursing home's physician's office, the dentist, the hearing aid dispenser, the ophthalmologist, the optometrist or the optician and the podiatrist? Sometimes you may have to take your loved one there to have necessary examinations, procedures, and fittings.

B. The general appearance of the facility

Look at the external building and grounds for general appearance. How well are the trees and shrubs maintained? Are they neatly trimmed? Where is the parking lot and are there ample parking spaces? Is it well lit at night? Do the doors and windows of the facility lock properly? This will provide you a clue on what the management of this facility is willing to do to assure that the surrounding is safe, neat and that overall, there is concern about the residents' environment.

II. Internal Environment
A. The initial impression

When you visit a facility, use your five senses (sight, hearing, smell, touch and taste) to determine the environment both inside and outside. Is there a strong urine odor or some other odor as soon as you enter the lobby? If such odor still exists by mid-morning or mid-afternoon, they usually imply that nursing care is substandard. You should also take note as to how the staff greet you. Are they attentive, courteous, sincere and friendly or are they rude, detached and aloof?

B. The attitude of the management team

Attitude is an important factor. It is the key to the quality of residents' care and the quality of a nursing home's environment. Are the attitudes of the Administrator or the Director of Nursing open and friendly, and do they show genuine concern for the care of the residents? Their attitudes will filter down to the staff and those in turn reflect on the residents' welfare.

C. The medical/rehabilitation aspect

This is obviously a principal consideration. Can this facility meet all the medical, nursing, physical, emotional, psychosocial and rehabilitation needs of your loved one?

The facility will have a list of all the available services. Arrange with the Administrator to interview with each of the department heads. Then be prepared to visit each and every department to try and assess if your loved one's needs can be met.

D. The General tour

Request to have a tour of the facility. If you get a sense that the facility's management personnel consider this request a burden, do not consider that facility further. They either truly do not care about what your concerns are, or they are too stressed out themselves to meet your needs and answer your questions. In either case, such a facility is "bad news". You should not waste your time, just leave.

Remember it is the staff inside the building who will be giving the care to the residents. Principally, this involves the nursing staff. Do they look satisfied on the job? Do they create a home-like atmosphere? Do the residents look happy and content?

E. Mandated postings

These are the postings that are required by the state and federal government licensing agencies. They are usually posted in a glass-enclosed bulletin board, either next to the lobby entrance, office of the Administrator or the office of the Director of Nursing. They will provide you with an idea of how the facility attends to the regulations and meets the goals set forth.

1. Look for postings of the facility licensing number, Administrator's licensing certificate number, telephone numbers of important government agencies, Ombudsman's name and telephone number, Medicare and Medicaid office numbers, a list of residents' rights and the statutory bill of rights.

2. Make sure that a copy of the <u>current year</u> state inspector's survey is available for you to read. This report

will identify the major deficiencies in the facility. You can also go to the state licensing and certification department to check on previous years' inspection reports. These reports will include the facility's stated plans to remove any cited deficiencies, and the deadline to comply with correcting the deficiencies. You should certainly find out if all these infractions have been corrected. Did any serious life-threatening (class A) deficiencies occur recently in this facility? You should be able to get this information from the Administrator or the Director of Nursing. Are these reports given to you freely or do they offer various excuses and act hesitant? Find out how many times the facility has been put on a "fast track" inspection by the State Department of Licensing and Certification Division. Being put on fast track usually means that the inspectors are concerned about the quality of care given to the residents. They will allow the facility a short period of time to correct these deficiencies. The inspectors can come back any time of the day or night. None of the facilities like to be put in that predicament. They will avoid this like a plague. In one instance with which I am familiar, one of the facilities of a large chain was put on fast track. The corporation had to send many extra staff there to give assistance. We had to work around the clock to correct all the deficiencies. It was not a very comfortable feeling.

Remember that even with all of the available documentations, do not base your decision solely on the reports because occasionally some bad nursing homes get good reports, and some good nursing homes get bad reports. Use your own intuition, judgment and assessments during your inspection tour.

F. "The tell-tale signs"[19]
1.   Request to see a resident's room and be sure to check the bathroom. Is there any urine odor as soon as you

---

[19]Weaver, P. & Spiropoulos, J., "The Right Way to Choose a Nursing Home", New Team Video, 1991.

walk into the resident's room or bathroom? Are the beds made neatly? Are the sheets and bedspreads clean and crisp, not flimsy? Are the night stands and the over-bed tables clean? Is there fresh water in a clean pitcher, and are there any clean cups?

2. Are all the residents up and in street clothes with matching socks and shoes, or are they sloppily dressed in hospital gowns? Again, this is not a hospital. It is a facility for the residents to recuperate and to live. Being dressed promotes an air of wellness, and that should be of concern to the staff. If some of the residents are in pajamas or in hospital gowns, find out why. Sometimes the residents request to be that way.

3. Do all the residents have clean, combed hair? Are the male residents shaved? Are female residents well-groomed? Are the residents' fingernails trimmed neatly? This is all part of the mission of such a facility: to promote wellness as much as possible. Any deficits in this area mean that the staff is either uncaring or the facility is so short staffed that they do not have the time to care. Both factors speak loudly about the overall ambiance of the facility.

4. Observe how the staff addresses the residents. Are they being treated with respect, with friendship, and with kindness? Do the staff converse with residents? Do all the staff members knock on the door before entering a resident's room? Do the staff call residents by their preferred names? Do you hear nicknames being used for the residents? The use of nicknames often construes disrespect for the elderly.

5. Are there any residents who are staying in bed all day? Who decides that "total bed rest" status and what are the criteria? In general, residents in a convalescent facility should not be in bed all day. They should at least be out of their rooms and in a wheelchair or a Geri-chair for a short duration each day.

6. Are some residents sitting hour after hour in a wheelchair or a Geri-chair without staff members changing their positions? Are they "parked" mindlessly in front a

television set, but they are not actually watching the program? Is the program that is turned on really to their interest or is it to the staff's needs? Are there other residents being parked in a corridor, where they are grabbing at anyone who passes by, yelling and crying for attention, or begging to be untied? What is the staff's response?

7. Observe how many of the residents who are sitting in wheelchairs have their feet dangling, unable to touch the footrest or floor? This is because facility's wheelchairs may be too high for some of the shorter residents. In this case, a concerned staff member would have placed a pillow on the footrest so that the resident's legs and feet are comfortably positioned.

8. How many residents are tied up in physical restraints to restrict movements? You should ask why they are being restrained. Another question to ask the staff or the Director of Nursing is: How many of the residents are being put on chemical restraints? These are mood and behavior altering drugs. Under most circumstances, the use of either physical or chemical restraints is against the law. These methods may only be used as a last resort and under well-documented physician's orders. We shall discuss both of these subjects in detail in another chapter.

G. Call bell:

Try and get a sense of the attentiveness of the staff to the needs of the residents. One of the best ways to check this point is to see if the call bell or some other alarm equipment is within easy reach of the residents regardless of where they are sitting or lying in bed. You should time the response time to the ringing of a call bell. A call bell, once pressed, should be answered within three to five minutes. This will give you a good idea about the quality of care.

H. Meal time

Walk through the dining hall at meal time and observe how the nursing assistants feed those residents who cannot handle this activity by themselves. Are they impatient? Do the staff seem to only talk among themselves, or do they talk with the residents they are feeding? Is there a licensed nurse stationed in the dining room during meal times in case there is an emergency? Request to have a meal with the residents so that you can taste the foods. Are the tray set-ups clean and neat? Is the food appealing to the appetite? What is the temperature of the hot and cold foods? Is there a dietitian supervisor, and can she be easily reached in time of need? What is her attitude toward you when you are asking your questions? Is there a possibility for a substitute meal in case an individual does not like a particular meal? Do the staff know how to calculate the percentage of food consumed?

I. Staffing adequacy

1. Staffing adequacies - This is a key point of concern. You must be on the lookout for not only adequacy in the number of staff per shift, but for the adequacy of training of the staff members. Are there Registered Nurses (RN) on duty eight hours a day, seven days per week. This also depends on the number of beds in the facility. If the facility is large (over one hundred beds), then there must be an RN on duty every shift. Are there Licensed Vocational Nurses (LVN) on duty twenty-four hours a day, seven days per week on all shifts? Ask to check the daily assignment sheet. Are all the nursing assistants certified by the state? Certified nursing assistants must sign their names on the assignment sheet followed by the acronym CNA. What is the residents-to-staff ratio? The federal OBRA regulations require that adequate staffing be provided in a nursing facility. This requirement stipulates that there shall be a 3.0 staffing hours per resident per day. To figure out if there is adequate staffing on any given 24-hour day, you can use this formula: Licensed nurses (RN + LVN) hours are counted as double hours and CNA hours counted as single hours. If you total these two numbers for the 24-hour period and divide that

number by the total resident census, you will obtain a number that can be compared with the one the state mandates as being the minimum care hours per resident per day. This number should be greater than 3.0 hours per resident per day to be considered adequate staffing. You should request to see several daily assignments sheet, especially the week-end ones, to ensure that these ratios have been adhered to consistently.

2. Visit the facility on an evening or even a night shift. An unannounced visit during a weekend or an evening will allow you to assess the quality of care given when the management team is not present. You can also check again on the resident-to-staff ratio.

3. Certified Nursing Assistant (CNA) assignments - You should ask if the CNAs are assigned to the same residents all the time or are they being rotated frequently. Continuity of care for the same residents will enhance quality of life and care. CNAs are most closely involved staff members with regard to daily functioning of the residents because they perform all of the bedside nursing care. They transfer information to the licensed nurses. The knowledge the CNAs have affects the welfare of the resident. It is very helpful if the CNAs are assigned to the same residents so that they get to know each resident well. Then any change in a resident's medical condition will be promptly noticed and reported to personnel higher up, i.e., the Nursing Supervisor or the Charge Nurses. Early medical intervention and treatments will prevent complications.

4. Nurse training sessions - For this information, you will have to talk to the Director of Staff Development (DSD). He or she will be able to provide you with the state-approved continuing education plans for the staff and precertification program for the nursing assistants. You should feel free to ask the DSD about his or her own qualifications to do that job. New nursing assistants must have fifty hours of theory and one hundred hours of clinical practice in order to be certified. Those who were on duty

prior to 1987 must nonetheless pass a special competency test put forth by the individual states. All CNAs must have twenty-four hours of continuing education every year in order to be recertified. Every new employee must have sixteen hours of comprehensive orientation before they can apply hands-on care to residents. Find out from the Director of Staff Development if this is carried out. All other department personnel must have twelve hours of inservice training per year in order to continue working in the facility.

J. The psychosocial aspects of living
    The activity programs are usually handled by the Director of Activities and others are handled by the Director of Social Services.
    1. Scheduling the activities - Since the facility is not just a hospital, there should be planned activities for the residents to participate, should they want to. You should look to see if there are scheduled activity programs daily for both men and women. How do the residents get to the location of activity programs if they are immobilized? Are there any alternative activity programs if the residents do not like the existing programs? How can residents set up new, alternative programs? Whom should they speak to? Are there any outings for the residents? How many volunteers come to the facility to perform music programs, dance recitals, or bingo games? Ask for at least two earlier activities schedules to see the variety of programming. Attend an activity program in progress. How well do they satisfy the needs of the residents?
    2. Council - Are there residents' council and family council? How are residents being notified of these scheduled meetings? If problems are presented at the council meeting, do they get resolved? Find out from the perspective of the members of these councils the facility's problems, the quality of nursing care, and the quality of life.
    3. Personal properties - Can residents bring their own furniture or belongings to the room? Can they have their

own telephone? Who is responsible for overseeing that other people will not tamper or misuse the phone brought in for the resident's own use?

4. Roommates - Can residents choose their own roommate? If not, what are the steps to take if roommates cannot get along? OBRA and State regulations require letters to be sent out to the resident and his/her family members for permission to move from one room to another.

5. Smoking policies - Nowadays many people know about the hazards of smoking. Not only is there the persistent danger of fire, but the smoke from cigarettes can be harmful to one's health and the health of those who live and work around the smoker. Nevertheless, smoking can be a habit that older people had acquired early in their lives and cannot give up. Questions relating to compatibility in smoking habit need to be answered: Are the residents allowed to smoke in their own room? If so, the facility is in serious violation against a fire code. Are there any designated smoking rooms or areas? What about roommates who do/do not smoke? What are the smoking schedules and is there any staff supervision for this activity? If cigarettes run out for a particular smoking resident, who is responsible for obtaining more for him/her? Where are privately purchased cigarettes being stored? If they are lost or come up short before replacement time, who will pay to replace them?

K. Additional Questions

1. Bed-hold policies - What is the policy for bed-hold when the resident has to be transferred to an acute hospital? Will his/her room still be available to him/her upon return? This is very important for residents who are on Medicaid. The state policy is that the facility must hold the bed for seven days. The family must notify the facility in twenty four hours about their intentions. If the family does not request it within those days then the bed may be taken up by others. The facility must also obtain an order from the physician for

the seven day bed-hold. Sometimes a physician with practicing privileges in that facility thinks that he/she is too overloaded. He/she may then opt to drop a resident who had gone to the acute hospital, especially if that individual is on straight Medicaid reimbursement.

2. Making the facility a home - Occasionally, a short-term resident decides not to return to his/her previous living environment and wants to make the nursing home his/her new permanent residence. If this happens to be the decision of your loved one, you may have to consider his/her other legal matters, finances, house, furniture, pets, and all other properties and assets. You can seek assistance from the business office or the Social Service Director. They can direct you to the appropriate personnel and agencies.

3. Choosing a physician - Once you have made a decision on the particular nursing home for your loved one, you should ask for a list of names of physicians who practice in that facility. From such a list, you can then choose one for your loved one.

The points highlighted in this chapter have provided the potential consumer a keener eye for the important criteria in choosing a quality nursing home facility. A choice based on your loved one's and your personal decisions that everyone is satisfied with the facility is a crucial one. Once that choice is made, you and your loved one will have to deal with the details of being admitted into that facility. These are the topics of the next two chapters.

CHAPTER 5

Admission and Transfer

The Initial Admission Inquiry...58
Admission Agreement Signatures..60
Patient/Facility Policies and Procedures Agreements..........61
Transfer...62
Important Forms to Sign for the Nursing Department.........67

We are now getting into the "heart of the matter" of convalescent hospital living. This is the broad topic of resident rights and the statutory bill of rights for nursing homes. This chapter and the following chapters will deal with several components of resident rights. At admission time, the new resident has many rights to be exercised, all aimed at how he/she wishes to be treated. There are rights regarding transfer and discharge, rights as a United States citizen and as a resident of the facility. There is the right to have a say in the use of physical and chemical restraints. Finally, there are the rights to good quality of life and high quality of care including medical, nursing, dietary and rehabilitation services, infection control, and a range of other items handled by the administration. We begin in this chapter with the admission process.

The initial admission inquiry between the acute hospital and the nursing facility:

You have now finished visiting and evaluating several facilities, and you have decided to place your loved one in one of them. It is important that you tell the Director of Nursing (DON) of that facility about your decision. This Director of Nursing will then contact the Patient Care

Coordinator (PCC) of the acute hospital to obtain all pertinent medical and physical information concerning your loved one's care. The initial admission inquiry form is a very comprehensive one. It includes: name, date of birth, name of the responsible party, payment status and the total picture of your loved one's mental and physical problems, medical diagnosis, medications, allergies, prior and current levels of activities of daily living, rehabilitation therapy services needed, and all other aspects of your loved one's psycho-social needs. Upon the completion of this form the Director of Nursing will meet with the "admission team" and will present the case for review. The question to be answered is, "Can this facility meet the needs of this prospective resident?" Most of the time, everyone agrees with the decision of the Director of Nursing to admit or not to admit. For those coming directly from the acute hospital, the question of how many more Medicare days of coverage are remaining is one that is also weighed by the facility's business staff. At this point, the Director of Nursing will notify the PCC again. She in turn will notify the responsible family member, and the process of transfer will be initiated. The first thing the PCC does is to conduct an assessment on Medicare PASSAR, evaluating the patient's mental status. If your loved one is on the federal Medicaid program, the PCC will also call the state and obtain prior authorization number for transfer .

The transfer from the acute hospital to the nursing home can be anything from an exciting adventure to a disaster. It all depends on your prior preparation with your loved one. A positive attitude, adequate preparation, love and understanding between you, your loved one, and all other family members, together with the conscientious help, patience, honesty, companionship and professional care of the nursing home staff, will make the uncertainty of life in a nursing home kept to a minimum. Be sure to let your loved one know that if this arrangement does not work out, you and the facility's social worker will look for other alternatives. Nowadays nursing home life can be a very rewarding experience particularly for a short stay and with rehabilitation as its sole purpose.

Admission agreement signatures:

The day prior to your loved one's admission, the nursing department will inform you what your loved one will need while living in the facility. We will return to this point in the chapters on the Quality of Life and the Quality of Care. On that same day prior to admission, the Medical Record Department or the business office manager of the nursing home will request for you, as the principal responsible person of your loved one, to come to the facility to sign the Admission Packet. The documents in this packet could take anywhere from one hour to two hours or longer to complete. The best thing to do is to take the Admission Packet home beforehand to read and understand all items thoroughly. On the day of signing, you and your loved one should take your time; do not let any staff member unduly rush you. Ask questions and obtain clarification as to the meanings of the paragraph wordings. Request to have enough time to absorb all the information necessary and to fully understand the respon-sibilities and rights of your loved one. All these items and forms are legal, binding contracts.

In the Admission Packet you will find these documents, some requiring your consent, others being informational: (Bold-face items will be further discussed in this chapter.)

Face sheet.

The Admission Packet: a very thick document.

Consent to medication and treatment.

CPR status consent form.

Durable Power of Attorney for Health Care.

Living Will.

Physical and Chemical restraint consent forms.

Pharmacy selection consent form.
Transfers.
Bed-Hold policy and Readmission consent.
Bedside Rails Consent Forms.
Resident Rights.
Durable Power of Attorney for finance.
Laundry services.
Clothing/Property Inventory, in the chart on
    the floor for nursing service to use.
Prior Stay Information.
Medicare Card and number, Part A effective
    date, and Part B, effective date.
    Medicare Questionnaire.
    Medicare denial letter.
Medicaid card and number - sometimes called
    the "POE sticker".
Medicaid information and Medicaid Formulary
    for drugs.
Social Security number.
Client Property Policy.

Patient/facility policies and procedures agreements:
    It is important to realize that in a nursing home
environment, your loved one will be subjected to various
policies and procedures that often seem to favor the
convenience of the facility over the dignity of your loved
one. The rules and regulations must be there if there is to be
any sense of order in the running of a complex organization.
Those admission agreements and other documents shall
ensure that each resident admitted to the facility has certain
obligations and responsibilities in addition to the rights
specified by regulations. They also clearly delineate duties
and responsibilities of the facility and its staff. When you
and your loved one are finally satisfied with all aspects of
these documents and have signed each of them, then a copy
of all signed material shall be given to the resident, or to you,
the responsible party.

Involvement of individual resident in admission:

OBRA regulations[20] clearly require facilities to invite the prospective client (your loved one) to participate in the admission process unless the person is judged to be incompetent, and/or the physician documents in writing that the client is incapable of signing the admissions contract. This regulation is sometimes hard to comply with due to the fact that often the prospective client is still in the acute hospital. After arrival to the convalescent facility, the new resident may be either too tired or too confused and disoriented to read and sign all these documents. Even the most competent person may sometimes elect not to be involved in the admissions process. Consequently, this important duty usually falls on the shoulders of the responsible party.

Transfer procedures from acute hospitals:

The acute hospital must provide sufficient preparation to ensure a smooth and safe transfer into the nursing facility for an extension of recovery care. Federal (OBRA) and state (in California it is called TITLE XXII) laws require that there is a doctor who will take over the care of the resident in the nursing home prior to admission and immediately after his/her admission. The nursing facility will give you or the patient care coordinator a list of the physicians who practice in this facility. The responsibility of getting a physician to care for your loved one usually belongs to you and the patient care coordinator. If there is no physician the nursing home facility will not be able to accept the prospective resident. The law also requires that a new resident must have a current medical history and a physical examination within the last five days. Either a tuberculosis skin test (PPD) or a chest x-ray within the last ninety days is

---

[20]Long Term Care Survey, The, American Health Care Association, Washington, D.C., 1992.

also necessary. At the time of admission, the facility also requires a written physician's discharge orders with diet, medications, treatment, activity programs, and rehabilitation therapy services explicitly stated. All this information usually comes automatically with him/her from the hospital. If an individual is coming from home, the responsibility of getting all the above information will be yours. If additional information from an acute hospital is necessary, then you or your loved one must sign a consent/release form to obtain this information from the hospital or from your physician's office. Without this critical information, the admission process can be held up even if you have a nursing home facility.

Admission policy:

There is widespread evidence that nursing home facilities actively discriminate against certain types of individuals. The two groups most at risk appear to be those individuals with heavy care needs and those whose primary source of payment is Medicaid. The evidence of this discrimination is varied. A report by the Committee on Nursing Home Regulation stated that the nursing home market is in fact two markets - a preferential one for those who can pay their own way (at market price) and a second, more restricted one, for those whose stays are paid by Medicaid[21] Nursing home administrators prefer to admit private pay residents over public pay residents because the Medicaid reimbursement rates are lower than charges to private pay residents. Nursing homes also want to select residents with relatively low levels of needs over the heavy care residents because those who require less care are less costly to care for. These residents will increase the profit margin for the owners. Because of these practices in the past,

---

[21]Committee on Nursing Home Regulation, Inst. of Medicine, Improving the quality of care in nursing homes. National Academy Press, Washington, 1986, p6.

the nursing homes now have to provide the following non-discriminatory policies to the new resident:

1. The facility must furnish to the new resident a written description of all the statutory bill of rights and resident rights while he/she is in the facility. These include:

   a. a description of how personal funds will be protected

   b. a description of the requirements and procedures for establishing eligibility for Medicaid

   c. a statement saying that the facility cannot request the spouse who is still living at home to use his or her resources or assets to pay the bills for the other spouse who is living in the facility

   d. a statement that the facility must post the names, addresses and telephone numbers of all pertinent State client advocacy groups including the State survey and certification agency, the State licensure office, the State ombudsman program, the protection and advocacy network, and the Medicaid fraud control unit

   e. a statement stating that the resident may file a complaint with the State survey and certification agency concerning resident abuse, neglect, and misappropriation of resident property while he/she is in the facility.

2. The facility must use identical policies regarding admission, transfer, discharge and services for all residents. Similarly, the facility must provide services under the federal and state plan for all individuals regardless of the source of payment and insurance health plans.

3. The facility cannot deny services to any person due to his or her age, handicap, race, color, national origin, ancestry, religion, or sex.

4. The facility must not require the residents to sign admission documents explicitly promising or agreeing not to apply for Medicare or Medicaid. It cannot require residents to pay private rates for a specific period of time before Medicaid will be accepted as a payment source of

the resident. The facility must not seek or receive any kind of assurance that the resident is not and will not ever be eligible for, or will not apply for, Medicare or Medicaid benefits.

5. The facility must not require a third party guarantee of payment to the facility as a consideration of admission, expedited admission, or continued stay in the facility. The facility may obtain legal financial access for payment from the resident's own income and resources but shall not cause personal financial liability on the part of the responsible party.

6. If a person is eligible for Medicaid, the facility must not charge, solicit, or receive from that individual any amount, in addition to those reimbursements received from the State, as a precondition of admission, expedited admission, or continued stay in the facility.

7. The facility may charge a Medicaid-eligible resident privately for items and services requested if Medicaid does not cover that specific item.

It should be noted that even with these stringent regulations, nursing homes still frequently fail to notify residents of their legal rights and sometimes even evict them illegally, according to a recent survey[22] released by Bet Tzedek Legal Services, a non-profit law firm representing the poor, the disabled and the elderly. In one case, a man was hauled off when Medicaid failed to pay his bill. The survey covered 65 nursing homes; nearly 92% of those residents who experienced involuntary discharge had been subjected to illegal tactics by the facility.

Skilled Nursing Facility's Admission procedure:

All nursing homes try to admit their new residents between the hours of 10 A.M. and 12 noon. By pushing the Patient Care Coordinator to transfer your loved one early on

---

[22]Carlson, Eric, "Nursing homes evict patients illegally, L.A. legal firm says". Sacramento Bee, May 13, 1995, p.B3.

the day of the discharge, you are giving the greatest amount of help to the nursing facility and allowing your loved one to settle in more comfortably. This process allows the nursing staff in the receiving facility to get in touch with the receiving physician to verify acute hospital physician's discharge orders and obtain new orders before the physician's office closes for two hours from noon to 2 P.M.. Do not leave the facility immediately after your loved one is in the facility. Make sure that you allow time to stay with him/her, and that he/she is relatively comfortable and calm before you leave the facility. It is also important to let him/her know the time when you will be back. Finally, do not give promises that will lead to false hopes.

The first day for the new resident in the nursing facility can be a real shocker. This is no longer just a visit; this is going to be his/her home for an extended period of time! He/she may see other residents sitting in wheelchairs and Geri-chairs. There may be residents yelling and screaming loudly. Other residents may be reaching out and gripping passers-by. There are even residents lying in bed making incomprehensible noises. Tell your loved one not to be afraid, because those residents are somebody else's loved ones too, and they also have feelings, needs and fears. In fact, on your next visit to the facility, when you pass these residents try to talk to them, touch them and even hug them. Your actions will be rewarded with a smile and a big hug in return.

As soon as your loved one has settled into his/her room, the nursing department and all other departments will come to conduct a comprehensive assessment. The resident is weighed, and his/her height is measured by the restorative aide, or by his or her own CNA for that day. The CNA will also list all his/her personal belongings on the clothing inventory list, and this list is then entered into the chart. He/she is also shown the location of the bathroom, the call bell, the closet, the dining room and the times that meals are served and the location of the activities calendar for the month. While the CNA is escorting your loved one around, the licensed staff is on the telephone verifying the admission orders with the resident's physician. Pharmacy is also called, and the drugs are ordered.

Important forms to sign for the Nursing Department
This section will concentrate on those parts of the admission agreement that concern the nursing care of your loved one. These forms must be signed before any nursing care can be administered. Those are the ones in bold-face print in our Admission Packet list:

I. CONSENT TO MEDICATION AND TREATMENT:
The OBRA regulation states that all residents who are admitted to the facility are under the direct supervision, medical treatment, and care of his or her own physician. The resident must give the staff of the facility permission to provide routine care as directed by that physician. If this form is not signed the staff cannot legally care for the resident.

Let me cite, from my personal experience, a case when a client refused to sign the papers: An alert and oriented Spanish speaking woman was transferred from an acute hospital to the skilled nursing facility because she had unresolved infections on both her legs and toes. She did not speak, read or understand English, and the acute hospital did not provide an interpreter for her to help her make the crucial decision concerning nursing home placement before her discharge. Her family members had informed the PCC of that hospital that they did not want to take care of her in their home, but no one, including the PCC, notified the patient about that decision. On the day of discharge she was put into a transfer van without any resistance because she thought that she was going to her daughter's family home. When she arrived at the skilled nursing facility, she refused to sign any admission papers even after the facility provided her with a Spanish speaking staff member to explain and to translate all the information to her. With her not willing to sign these consent forms the facility could not legally touch her. When she asked to have a drink of water and to use the bathroom, the staff legally could not comply with her wishes. There was a distinct possibility that this lady could have ended up outside the facility. Fortunately the staff in this facility was very caring, and one of them went to the Administrator and received permission to provide temporary care to this patient. The state Ombudsman was also called for assistance. After many hours of inter-facility negotiations between the administrative personnel of this facility and the originating hospital, the woman was transferred back to the acute hospital.

II. The CPR status (preferred intensity of care):

The acronym CPR stands for CARDIO (heart), PULMONARY (lung) RESUSCITATION (compression). CPR is the standard resuscitation practice when a person stops breathing and his/her heart stops beating. Usually when a person stops breathing, his/her heart will also stop beating within a few minutes. CPR is a two-step procedure. The first step is mouth-to-mouth resuscitation to blow oxygen into the lungs. The second step is external compression of the heart to maintain circulation to all the vital organs. A form consenting to or denying the use of CPR must be signed at the time of admission. Be sure your loved one, you, as the primary responsible party and the rest of your family members discuss this important issue at home before any crisis arises. When you are at the hospital discuss it with your primary physician when all concerned members are present. You, your loved one, and all your family members must understand and agree on all the statements and ramifications as stated in this "preferred intensity of care" form. Otherwise when an emergency arises, conflict will result between your loved one, you, your family members, and the physician.

There has been a recent study on the senior citizen's view of using CPR.[23] When 371 patients in a senior health center were surveyed, initially 41% said they would like to have CPR under the conditions spelled out above. However, when informed that for seniors, the chances of surviving are only between 10 to 17%, only 22% of the seniors stilled opted for having CPR.

The decision for having CPR performed or not performed is not irrevocable. In the convalescent hospital, this form must be updated every six months by the physician after a thorough discussion with the resident or his/her family. This allows you or your loved one to change your mind or to keep the previous agreement. To check the box that says to "have CPR" means that you want everything done for your loved one after he/she has stopped breathing and his/her heart has stopped beating. This procedure must start within four to six minutes after the heart stops beating. If more time than that has elapsed, there is a chance of irreversible brain damage. That means even if he/she were brought back to life, he/she may end up living in a "vegetative state", totally unresponsive and stripped of all life's dignity. Since time is of an essence, given a "yes" on the CPR form, the facility's staff will start CPR and call 911 immediately if a resident is found to be in a state requiring the procedure. When the paramedics arrive at the facility, they will start intubation, IV therapy, administer emergency medications, connect you loved one to an EKG monitor, defibrillate if there is ventricular fibrillation (irregular heart beat that results in death), and perform any other orders that the paramedics receive from the emergency room physician of the acute hospital. This procedure is continued all the way to the hospital even if there is no breathing or heart beat for

---

[23]Abstracted from Murphy, D.J., et al., The Influence of the Probability of Survival on Patients' Preferences Regarding Cardiopulmonary Resuscitation, *New England J. Medicine*, 330: 545-549, 1994. (Copyrighted 1994. Massachusetts Medical Society. All rights reserved.)

an extended period of time. When your loved one arrives at the acute hospital all heroic measures will continue to be applied. If the heart beat returns, he/she will eventually be admitted to the intensive care unit and connected to a life support machine. The ability to recover at this stage depends upon the person's age, the severity of the illness, and the will to live.

To check the box that says "NO" to CPR means that you do not want any heroic measures taken when your loved one stops breathing or his/her heart stops beating. It also means that you want your loved one to die peacefully. You can still request all the comfort measures to alleviate suffering and to preserve dignity. These measures can include the use of antibiotics, the use of a nasogastric tube, the use of prescribed pain killers, transfer to an acute care hospital, application of oxygen, the use of suction and the insertion of an indwelling foley catheter. You can also request that your loved one not be transferred to an acute hospital so that he/she can die in a familiar environment, in his/her own bed and own room, surrounded by familiar staff personnel. Be sure to list all your requests on this form specifying exactly what you want. If there is a need to change this decision, simply discuss this need with your physician first, then go to the medical records or business office to request a new form and sign it correctly with the new decision. Be sure you keep a copy of the form that you signed. Should a resident with intact mental status utter in his/her last breath, "I do not want to die." or "Help me live." then the preferred intensity of care form "NO CPR" will in effect have been over-ridden. The staff must then call the doctor immediately and do everything possible to save the life of the resident. Therefore it is very important to discuss this matter thoroughly with your loved one. Be sure that everyone in your family understands the implications of the CPR consent and is in total agreement.

III. The DURABLE POWER OF ATTORNEY FOR HEALTH CARE:

The essence of this form is that an individual who initiates such a form has designated someone who he/she trusts to carry out the wishes of his/her individual medical care if and when he/she is totally incapacitated and rendered mentally or physically incompetent. A patient/resident in good health who is mentally competent can designate another person to make critical health decisions in his/her place, knowing that the decisions will be legally binding.

IV. LIVING WILL:

This is a legal document in which a person proclaims the desire to be allowed to die a natural death when he/she is in a state of permanent coma or a life of poor quality that cannot be improved. Physicians must discuss very clearly and precisely these directives with the resident, the responsible party and other family members. In the state of California, the living will is called "THE CALIFORNIA NATURAL DEATH ACT", and the signed Will is called a DECLARATION. When one signs this declaration, it instructs the physician that he/she does not want any treatment that would only prolong the time of his/her dying. All life-sustaining treatment would be stopped if he/she were terminally ill, his/her death was expected soon, or if he/she were permanently unconscious. The individual would still receive treatment to keep him/her comfortable. In making this declaration known to one's doctor, the physician is obligated to follow the wishes about limiting treatment. No one can change this legal document. It goes without further elaboration that the physician should definitely be made known of this decision and a copy of the signed form should be left with him/her. This form gives them (designee and physician) legal protection when they follow this individual's wishes. Some advance directives specify the type of treatment to be avoided. Others simply state the desire to avoid heroic or extraordinary measures. It grants the proxy the right to make certain decisions about the dying individual. This document pertains specifically to health care decisions in that it takes effect while the individual is still alive, but has become unable to think for himself.

V. PHYSICAL AND CHEMICAL RESTRAINT FORMS:

If you do not want your loved one to have any physical or chemical restraints applied on him/her, then sign this form. Do not let the facility's personnel talk you into a "yes" on this form without a reasonable and thorough assessment. Since it takes an individual approximately twenty-one days to adjust to any new environment, postponing this decision until the adjustment period has passed is all right. The topics of these restraints are of such importance that they will be dealt with in depth in separate chapters later.

VI. BEDSIDE RAILS CONSENT FORM:

If you or your loved one thinks that the bedside rails do not constitute too much of a physical restraint during night time, and if you think that the sense of safety for your loved one outweighs the inconvenience of releasing the rails before getting off the bed, then you should sign "YES" on this form. The only potential drawback of these rails lies with those residents who like to climb. In that case, the higher rail simply means a harder fall, and that is ill-affordable.

VII. PHARMACY:

You have the choice of using the facility's designated pharmacy or you may indicate on the form your personal preference. The problem with a privately chosen pharmacy arises when your loved one becomes ill and requires an antibiotic or other medication during evening hours or in the middle of the night. The law requires the facility to give the first dose of an antibiotic within four hours after receiving the order. If it is considered a "Stat" order (immediately), the time limit is only one hour. Since a regular pharmacy that does not supply convalescent hospitals usually will not deliver medication or supplies on demand, or remain open after certain hours in the evening, the nursing staff will have to call you to go to your chosen pharmacy to pick up the necessary drugs. This could leave you in a bind. If the facility does not receive the medication on time the staff will have to call the facility's own pharmacy to cover the drug, and in turn the pharmacy will bill you privately both for transportation and the price for the medication. This process can become an expensive venture. Since there is no obvious advantage for using private pharmacies, the case for recommending the use of the facility's pharmacy to avoid this headache is a strong one.

VIII. TRANSFERS AFTER ADMISSION:

After entering a nursing facility, there are several reasons why your loved one may be transferred to another facility. These are:

1. The resident's acute medical needs cannot be met in that facility. If transfer is due to a significant change in the resident's condition, then prior to any action, the facility must conduct an appropriate assessment of that medical condition unless the change is of an emergency nature requiring immediate attention.

2. The resident's health has improved sufficiently so he/she can go to a lower level of care.

3. The safety of that individual in the facility is endangered.

4. The health of individuals other than your loved one in the facility would otherwise be endangered. An example of this would be if a resident has a tendency to strike or molest other weaker residents.

5. The resident has failed, after reasonable and appropriate notice, to pay for the stay in the facility.

6. The facility ceases to operate.

On all the above transfers except #1 a written notice must be sent to the family thirty days before the discharge with the reason for the transfer, right to appeal, information on how to notify the Ombudsman, and information on how to notify the appropriate protection and advocacy agency for residents with mental illness or mental retardation. If the transfer is an emergency, the family is telephoned first, and a written notice is sent within twenty-four hours of the transfer. Every transfer to an acute hospital must have a duplicate inter-facility transfer sheet.

IX. BED-HOLD POLICY AND RE-ADMISSION:
1. To and from an acute hospital

When a nursing facility transfers a resident to an acute hospital, the staff must notify the family both orally and in writing that it is the policy of the facility to honor your loved one's bed-hold for seven days. If you want your loved one to return to this facility, an order must be obtained from the physician to accompany him/her. If the resident's condition is such that there needs to be a more extended stay in the acute hospital, then the facility has the right to fill the bed with a new resident after seven days. However, if the facility was notified by you or your physician beforehand of the prolonged acute hospital stay, then the facility must readmit him/her to the first available bed when he/she is able to return.

2. Leave of absence

If you decide to take your loved one home for a therapeutic leave of absence over a weekend, you must bring him/her back within three days unless other arrangements have been made previously. Even though there are no regulations governing these leaves of absence, most facilities have, as matter of policy, a three-day bed-hold for LOA residents. So whenever there is uncertainty as to the time of return, please notify the facility in advance for an extension of that leave, otherwise the facility may fill that empty bed. For an individual completely dependent on Medicaid, the law allows eleven LOAs in a month. If he/she exceeds this number, it may mean that he/she does not require skilled nursing facility care. A lower level of care would be more appropriate.

As a general rule, if a resident has an outstanding Medicaid balance, the law forbids the facility from keeping that resident out permanently when he/she is on a leave either to an acute hospital or to home. Once readmitted, however, this resident may be transferred if the facility can demonstrate that non-payment of charges exists and the proper documentation and notice requirement are followed. If on the other hand, your loved one is on Medicare Part A coverage, do not take him/her out of the facility for any outing. Once gone, your loved one will immediately forfeit the coverage. For those on a private-pay basis, the facility will refund any part of your loved one's stay away from the facility if you or your loved one decides not to return. Otherwise, your pre-payment will go toward the bed-hold. Further detailed clarification of the rules of coverage by insurance agents (Medicare, Medicaid or private) is discussed in the next chapter.

CHAPTER 6

Financing Nursing Home Care

Medicare..77
    Medicare Part A , SNF Coverage...............................79
    Medicare Part B...87
Medicaid..90
Private Insurance...92

In this chapter the discussion will be on the financial aspect and available health insurance plans for a person who is planning to enter or contemplating placing a loved one into a nursing home. Everyone worries that one's lifetime savings will not be enough for the long-term nursing home care expenses. Unfortunately, usually this is very true. Today, a nursing home stay averages $30,000 to $50,000 a year. This is beyond the financial reach of most individuals and families. There are basically just two ways to bear this burden: be very rich or be very poor. If you are fortunate enough to be rich, you can buy any service you need or want. On the other hand, if you are very poor, the state will support you for life. However, for the majority of people who are part of the middle or working class, when nursing home care becomes necessary, they are neither rich enough to support themselves nor poor enough to qualify for public assistance. This may well be the first time that they face the prospects of poverty. This feeling of inadequacy, and the loss of pride, self-esteem and dignity that comes with it, often go hand in hand with the real financial concern.

One of the forms that you have read and signed prior to or at the time of admission says that if your loved one's assets run out during his/her stay, the facility will notify you that within thirty days your loved one will have to either make other financial arrangements or move out. If out of pride and vanity you refuse to apply for public assistance (Medicaid) for your loved one, then when you or your loved one really can no longer afford the services of the nursing home, he/she will be out of a place to stay. The crucial questions you have to consider are: Should I and my loved one swallow our pride and accept long term care through Medicaid assistance? Will having accepted this public assistance cause any difference in the manner that my loved one is treated in the facility? (In principle, the answer to this question is an absolute "no".) Finally, what other preventive measures are available so that one does not go into a state of poverty? In this chapter, Medicare benefits for specific skilled nursing care will be the point of focus. It will be followed by an explanation of what Medicaid is, and finally how some people are able to escape poverty by innovative private insurance programs.

MEDICARE   (FEDERAL   HEALTH   INSURANCE PROGRAM)

Medicare is a program for people age 65 or older and for people under 65 who have received disability benefits for at least two years. It was established in 1965 under Title XVIII of the Social Security Act. It is administrated by the federal government's Health Care Financing Administration (HCFA). Its intent is to provide the elderly population easy accessibility to quality health care. In some respects, Medicare can be considered a form of national health insurance. When you retire and receive your Social Security benefits, your Medicare Part A (hospital coverage) will be activated automatically.[24] The annual cost of Medicare/ Medicaid reimbursements for nursing home care amounts to roughly 31 billion dollars. In the state of California, of all nursing home cost reimbursements, Medicare accounts for only between 2 to 4%, while Medicaid insurance (to be

---

[24]*Medicare 1994 Handbook, The,* HCFA, US DHHS

discussed later) accounts for up to 63.5%.[25] The remaining costs are met almost completely by private payments. Although small in percentages, Medicare does play an essential role in the nursing home industry.

Medicare benefits are payable from two funds:

PART A services are reimbursed from funds derived from the payroll tax. The actual distribution of money and sorting of claims are done by third-party payers to hospitals and physicians. Organizations handling claims from hospitals, skilled nursing facilities, and home health agencies are called **intermediaries** with whom the government has signed a contract. In California they are Mutual of Omaha and Blue Cross/Blue Shield of California. Organizations and companies handling claims for durable medical supplies (such as hospital beds, oxygen equipment or wheelchairs) are called **carriers.**

PART B services are reimbursed from a fund created by voluntary premium payments and general revenues. It pays for medically necessary physician's services, outpatient services and other medical services and supplies that are not covered by PART A. You must pay a deductible and coinsurance. In 1994, you must pay the first $100 in approved charges for covered medical expenses. This is called the Medicare Part B annual deductible. You only have to meet this once during the year. After you pay the annual deductible, you will own a share of the Medicare-approved amount for most services and supplies. This share is called coinsurance. Usually your coinsurance is 20 percent of the Medicare-approved amount.

Three additional terms you should be familiar are: 1. benefit days, 2. reserve days, and 3. Medigap insurance.

---

[25]Fleck, Barbara, Modern rest homes have new image. *Daily Democrat, The,* Woodland, CA, June 25, 1995, p.1.

I. Benefit period: A benefit period is the duration of time you are using services under Medicare Part A. Your first benefit period begins the first day you receive acute inpatient hospital care. Your benefits period ends after you leave the hospital or you have not received any skilled nursing or rehabilitation services for 60 days in a row. After one benefit period has ended, another one can start anew whenever you enter the hospital as an inpatient with a new diagnosis. Each benefit period can be as long as 90 days.

II. Reserve days: If you have to stay longer than the 90 days, Medicare will be able to cover a number of those days. These extra days are called reserve days. You have only 60 reserve days in your lifetime. Once you use this up, it cannot be restored. If you do not want to use your reserve days, you must inform the hospital in writing, either when you are admitted to the hospital or up to 90 days after discharge. If you use reserved days and then decide that you did not want to use them, you must request approval from the hospital to get them restored.

III. Medigap insurance: When an individual has exhausted his/her Medicare Part A, Medigap insurance may occasionally help to extend coverage for medically necessary covered services in a skilled nursing facility. However, the following rules apply:
1. You must be 65 or older and are enrolled in Medicare for the first time, based on age rather than on disability.
2. You apply for Medigap within 6 months of enrollment in Part B.

All Medigap policies must be standardized, and they should include the core policy package. Medigap coverage is such that you have to pay a co-payment after a certain number of days.

MEDICARE PART A COVERAGE IN SKILLED NURSING HOMES:

After your loved one's acute stage of illness is stabilized and he/she still need an extension period to recover, Medicare <u>Part A</u> will help pay for his/her care in a <u>Medicare-participating</u> skilled nursing facility if the individual meets all of these five conditions:

1. Your loved one's condition requires daily skilled nursing or skilled rehabilitation services which can only be provided in a skilled nursing facility.

2. Your loved one had been in an acute hospital at least <u>three days</u> in a row (not counting the day of discharge) before he/she is admitted to a participating skilled nursing facility.

3. Your loved one is admitted to the facility within 30 days after he/she leaves the acute hospital.

4. Your loved one's care in the skilled nursing facility is for a condition that was treated in the acute hospital, or for a condition that arose while he/she was receiving care in the skilled nursing facility for a condition which was treated in the hospital.

5. A physician certifies that your loved one's needs, and can benefit from receiving skilled nursing or skilled rehabilitation services **on a daily basis.**

Many people think that they are automatically entitled to get 100 days of Medicare coverage after discharge from the hospital and upon entering a skilled nursing facility. This is not true. Each new admission is judged by the above five conditions. Sometimes your loved one will not qualify for any further skilled care or rehabilitation services because the acute hospital's nursing and rehabilitation team have already tried everything humanly possible, but unsuccessfully, to get your loved one to progress to a partial or full level of independence. In such a situation, the skilled nursing facility may still do an independent assessment and decide from there whether rehabilitation in the SNF is going to be beneficial to your loved one. Sometimes the staff in skilled nursing facilities have a very hard time making family members understand the difference between an extended care and custodial care (long-term care). Medicare coverage is solely directed toward <u>extended</u> care, care that may have a reasonable chance for success in terms of rehabilitation potential. The name extended care really means an extension of care for the illness that had sent the person to the acute hospital initially.

Skilled nursing care are those services that require a registered nurse's experiences and training, a physical therapist's knowledge and skills because the resident's condition and needs are too complex, too unpredictable, or too serious and too unstable to be left to other less specialized staff to take care alone. All these skilled services must be considered reasonable, necessary and practical in terms of their duration and quality for recovery. If after the facility's professional assessment shows that there are indeed needs, then Medicare will help pay for up to 100 days of medically necessary and reasonable care in each benefit period. Medicare will <u>not</u> cover the care if it is mainly custodial in nature: eating, taking routine medications by mouth, walking, getting in and out of bed or chair, bathing, dressing, grooming, and toileting. These services could be provided by persons without the specialized professional skill or training that the staff of a skilled nursing facility have.

The average length of rehabilitation services that is paid for by Medicare usually is between two to four weeks. Occasionally, skilled nursing services can go up to the limiting 100 days (like a resident with a new naso-gastric/gastrostomy tube feeding). There are guidelines on approximately how many days Medicare will pay for each medical condition. Nowadays all newly admitted residents should be able to qualify for at least fourteen to twenty-one days of Medicare coverage because of the new comprehensive resident assessment instrument (the MDS).

Of all the nursing home reimbursements, Medicare skilled nursing care payment constitutes a very limited amount. Today, less than two percent of nursing home services are paid for by Medicare. The Medigap Supplement is thought by many to fill the gap between the actual cost of a long-term care stay and what Medicare does not pay. This is again not true since Medigap Supplement will only pay benefits if the individual qualifies for Medicare.

If your loved one does qualify for Medicare payment in a SNF, then the benefits he/she receives will cover:

1. A semiprivate room.
2. All his/her meals, including special diets.
3. Regular nursing services.
4. Physical, occupational, and speech therapy.
5. Drugs furnished by the facility during his/her stay.
6. Blood transfusions furnished during his/her stay.
7. Medical supplies such as dressings, splints and casts furnished by the facility.
8. Use of durable medical supplies such as a wheelchair or a walker.

Skilled nursing observation and assessment in a SNF will include care for the following items:

1. Difficulty in breathing.
2. Edema (swelling).
3. Bleeding.
4. Nausea.
5. Infection.
6. Suction need.
7. Wound status.
8. Activity tolerance.
9. Symptom returns.
10. Response to new medications.
11. Vital signs.

Skilled nursing services include:

1. Bowel and bladder retraining programs. This requires a physician's order and the interdisciplinary team's assessment and cooperation before the program can begin.
2. Special cast care - orthopedic traction.
3. Chemotherapy and radiation therapy- terminal care.

4. Newly post-operative colostomy and ileostomy care and teaching.
5. Stage III or IV pressure sores and multiple stage II skin problems care.
6. Sterile dressing changes.
7. Nasogastric or gastrostomy tube feedings.
8. Medications by subcutaneous, intramuscular, or intravenous injections.
9. Tracheotomy care, suctioning and respiratory care including initial positive pressure   breathing (IPPB) treatment.
10. Post-cataract surgery care including frequent use of eye drops.
11. Prosthetic device usage.
12. Catheterchanges and insertions of individual sterile irrigation to prevent infection.
13. Minimum Data Set assessment.
14. Patient education for newly diagnosed brittle diabetics' insulin injection.

Rehabilitation services include the following:
1. **Physical therapist** will retrain the individual for his/her gait, for balance, for building body strength, for learning transfer technique, and for increasing the range of motion and ambulation. The therapist will concentrate on the functions of the lower extremities (gross muscle movements).
2. **Occupational therapist** will concentrate on the functions of the upper extremities such as using assistive devices to eat, to dress, and to relearn how to do one's own ADL care. These are considered fine muscle movements.
3. **Speech therapist** teaches your loved one how to do strengthening exercises in the mouth, relearn how to talk, and how to swallow without choking.

The schedule of Medicare payment for the above services is:

1. The first 20 days Medicare pays all services.
2. From 21 through 100 days Medicare pays all services except $87.00 per day.
3. After 100 days you have to pay for all the services. If your loved one is on Medicaid already, then this will automatically take over.

When your loved one is on Medicare coverage, he/she must be facility bound. He/she cannot go out for an entertainment outing (eating in a restaurant) or visit family or friends on weekends. If he/she does these activities, then he/she is considered not sick enough to require the daily skilled nursing care or rehabilitation services, and Medicare coverage will immediately stop.

An example: A resident went home after an extend illness from the acute hospital. The family thought they could take care of her at home. But after an exhausted week of 24-hour, round-the-clock care, they transferred her to a nursing home for more extensive skilled nursing care and rehabilitation services. The resident and her family were very cordial, friendly and extremely cooperative. She was put on Medicare coverage because of her unstable condition and need for skilled nursing care and rehabilitation services. The administration further explained to her that she must remain in the facility (facility-bound) in order to be on Medicare coverage. The resident and her family agreed. After a few days her condition improved and she felt much better. She decided to go out for her outing against all the advice given by the facility. The end result was she lost her Medicare coverage.

DENIAL:
There are three type of Medicare denials: 1. facility denial, 2. utilization review committee denial, and 3. Medicare intermediary denial.

I. Facility denial:

If the facility's Director of Nurses, after reviewing the nurses' notes and all other professional staff's notes, decides that your loved one no longer needs the level of skilled nursing care covered by Medicare, she can issue a facility denial. The facility must notify you of this decision immediately. If you disagree with this decision, the facility must submit your claim at your request to Medicare for an official Medicare decision on coverage. The facility may not require you to pay a deposit until Medicare issues its decision. You must pay for any coinsurance while your claim is being processed, and for any services which are never covered by Medicare. The Director of Nursing must bring the case before the next Utilization Review Committee (URC) meeting for further review. Sometimes the URC can overturn the decision, but not vice versa.

II. Utilization Review Committee denial:
Every facility that participates in Medicare and Medicaid services must have a Utilization Review Committee. It is mandated by the federal government's Medicare program. The committee members consist of at least three physicians (the Medical Director, who may or may not be the resident's own physician [with no voting right] and two other physicians who do not have patients/residents in the facility), the Administrator, the Director of Nursing, the Director of Staff Development (who is also responsible for infection control), the Office Manager, the Pharmacist, and the Rehabilitation Therapists. The purposes of this committee are to decide whether an individual resident qualifies for Medicare coverage, to prepare studies of patterns of care, and to determine appropriate cost effectiveness of care.
All Medicare residents must be presented by the Director of Nursing to the URC every month for recertification or denial. Information presented include the medical record number, the diagnosis, date of admission, transferring hospital, and a detailed description of the

medical, nursing, and rehabilitation services the resident is receiving, and the level of progress in each. She cannot interject her opinion or bias the committee members' decision. If there are any questions to be clarified, she will present further information from the chart. If the committee approves or denies the care, at least two physicians (excluding the resident's own physician) must sign the report. All deliberations are held in the strictest of confidence. However, when the URC members deny Medicare coverage a letter must be sent immediately to notify the resident, the family, and the resident's own physician indicating the reason for denial. The resident has a three day grace period for coverage. This allows the resident or his/her family time to agree or disagree with the decision, and also gives him/her time to look for other sources of payment. If a resident or his/her responsible party decide to disagree, the facility must submit an appeal at his/her request to Medicare for an official Medicare decision on coverage.

III. Medicare Intermediary denial:

Medicare intermediary denials are often based on one of four problems: (1) failure of the resident to progress, (2) the specific stay of the resident is considered to be unreasonable and unnecessary for the diagnosis or treatment of an illness or injury, (3) poor and conflicting documentation between nurses and therapists, and (4) the documentation sent was not specific enough to qualify that resident for Medicare services. Both the resident and the facility will receive a copy of the denial letter from the Medicare office if any of these problems arise. If the resident receives such a letter, he/she should take the letter to the facility immediately and contact the Director of Nursing and the business office manager for further assistance.

At this juncture, both the resident (or his/her responsible party) and the facility will have to initiate appeals to the Medicare office. The facility must fill out an

MRQ (Medicare Review Questionnaire) to justify the needed services during that benefit period. In the meantime, the resident has to: 1. ask his/her medical provider to get an official Medicare determination, and 2. this provider must file a claim on the resident's behalf to Medicare. The resident will then get a Notice of Utilization from Medicare. This notice is the official Medicare determination of this appeal. If the facility has a record of low denial rate Medicare will go ahead and pay for these inappropriately filled-out claims.

MEDICARE PART A NON-COVERED SERVICES:

Examples of care deemed to be not reasonable and necessary include:

1. When a patient is placed in a skilled nursing facility when his/her care could be provided elsewhere.

2. If a patient's stay in a hospital or skilled nursing facility is longer than the duration considered to be "reasonable and necessary".

3. Personal convenience items, private duty nurses, and extra charges for a private room.

4. If a doctor comes to treat a patient or the patient visits him/her for treatment more often than is the usual medical practice in the area. Medicare will make exceptions to this rule if there are medical complications requiring more frequent physician visits.

It is important to note that all other "third party" health insurance payers will follow Medicare regulations and guidelines they also will not cover the type of care considered not reasonable or necessary. Be sure to read the fine print in the policy carefully to find out what is included before signing up for other insurance policies. Otherwise you may find yourself having to pay a huge bill in addition to the new premium.

MEDICARE PART B COVERAGE:

As previously mentioned, Medicare Part B is a voluntary participation part of the Medicare program. Under this program, you must pay annual premiums and deductibles. Then at the expiration of <u>Part A</u> benefits, Medicare <u>Part B</u> will kick in. Medicare <u>Part B</u> will pay 80 percent of the reasonable charges for covered services. Please keep in mind that not all individuals will be covered for all services listed below. Each will require an assessment and a doctor's order. This plan covers outpatient laboratory services, outpatient x-ray programs, outpatient physical therapy, occupational therapy and speech therapy services, wound care kits, incontinence care supplies, postural support devices, and a number of other medical services and supplies that are not covered by Medicare <u>Part A</u>. Some of the services that are not covered under <u>Part B</u> are: routine physical examinations and tests, routine foot care, eye and hearing exams for prescribing or fitting eyeglasses or hearing aids, dental care and immunizations.

Millions of older Americans go without their prescription drugs because they are either non-compliant or they can not afford to pay for them. Fortunately some drug companies offer free medication to poor and poorly insured persons. There are eligibility requirements for this program. Low-income seniors with drug coverage under Medicaid would not qualify for most programs. If you think that you might qualify for this assistance, you can get a list of participating pharmaceutical companies from the magazine called *Secure Retirement*, the official publication of the National Committee to Preserve Social security and Medicare. You can find the address and phone number at the end of this chapter. You may take the list to your physician and ask if he/she will call the company that manufactures the drugs you need. The physician must determine which company manufactures the needed drug. Then he/she must find it on the list and call the program. When approved, the medication is sent directly to the physician's office. If the manufacturer is not on the list, it does not mean they do not have the program. Request your physician to call the sales representative of the company to find out. Do not contact the companies yourself.

Assistance for Low-Income Beneficiaries:

Since Medicare is a federally mandated hospital and medical insurance program, there is a premium that must be paid by the individuals. The premium is attached to the hospital deductible and coinsurance. Sometimes, for an elderly citizen, this premium payment becomes a hardship. For such citizens, this premium can be paid through the associated Medicaid program. The Honorable Henry A. Waxman, Representative in Congress from the State of California, said:

"As of January 1, 1991, all Medicare beneficiaries with income below 100 percent of federal poverty level, which is $6,620 per year for an individual, and assets, other than a home or a car, less than $4000 are entitled to have Medicaid pick up the cost of their Medicare premium, deductibles and co-insurance.

The problem is that millions of poor seniors appear not to be getting this benefit. A report issued last month by Families USA found that over 2 million poor seniors are not receiving this due protection. This means that every month $29.90 is being deducted from the Social Security checks of those low income beneficiaries, people who the Congress expressly directed to protect from those losses."[26]

In California, a Families USA study estimated that some 250,000 seniors meet the eligibility criteria for the buy-in protection against Medicare cost-sharing, but only about

---

[26]Waxman, Hon. Henry A, Congressman from California, Subcommittee on Oversight & Investigations of the Committee on Energy & Commerce. U.S. House of Representatives, 102nd Congress. Serial No. 102-91, p.198, 1992.

one-tenth of this population is actually receiving this benefit.[27]

In order to qualify for this premium write-off, the annual income level must be near the national poverty guidelines. Poverty guidelines are set at $6,810 for one person and $9,190 for a family of two. You cannot have resources such as bank accounts or stocks and bonds worth more than $4,000 for an individual or $6,000 for a couple. Your personal home, car, furniture, jewelry, or life insurance need not be counted in this means test.

Eligibility determination now must be made by Medicaid services and not by the Social Security district office. Be sure to check with the County Welfare Department for further information. Your loved one is entitled to this benefit.

MEDICAID (Welfare) BENEFICIARIES:

Medicaid (welfare) is a joint venture of the federal and state governments designed to provide assistance to the low income, poverty stricken population. It is administered by the state under broad federal guidelines. This is the major and the largest source of public reimbursement covering more than half of nursing home services' bills. The program is administered by the Health and Welfare Division of each state that licenses nursing homes, certifies clients for coverage, sets the rate of payment to the nursing homes based on financial needs, and enforces regulations to participating homes. Each state sets its own eligibility requirements. The aspect that is most disturbing about this program is that the insured must be below the poverty level in order to qualify for benefits.[28]

Many people try to circumvent this problem by "spending down" their assets before they get sick, or by

---

[27]Families USA study, as reported by Waxman, H.A., (cf. footnote 26).
[28]Budish, Armond D., 1994. *Avoiding the Medicaid Trap: How to Beat the Catastrophic Costs of Nursing Home Care*, Henry Holt and Co. New York.

selling their house and other major assets to their children for a few dollars. This means that the person must "spend down" their asset to a base of approximately $2,000 total excluding the home and automobile. Once having satisfied this criterion of poverty, Medicaid will pay for nursing home's custodial care, provided the nursing home is certified.

It should be noted, however, to be eligible for Medicaid coverage, you cannot spend down within three years of applying or entering a nursing home. Furthermore, new regulations have now been put into effect to discourage spending-down in the form of gifts to one's own relatives. Most states have a "look-back" clause to see how much was given as a gift to a relative. For each dollar given as a "gift", the state can disqualify the giver an equivalent number of days before Medicaid comes into effect. For example: Your loved one had given you a sum of $150,000 prior to his/her entering the nursing home. He/she then applies for Medicaid benefits. When the state examines the record and finds that the gift to you is solely for the purpose of becoming impoverished in name only, but not in fact, so as to get onto welfare, it will estimate that at a rate of $3,000 per month nursing home cost, your loved one will not be eligible for Medicaid benefits for 50 months after he/she initiates that application. In other words, the state expects that the burden of nursing home care must be shared between the state and the individual. The state is to be the participant only as a last resort: true poverty.

For a skilled nursing facility, Medicaid certification means that it meets a stringent set of government standards, e.g., OBRA and state regulations. In California, they are the regulations under Title XXII. The reimbursement rate per day of care is also set by the individual state. This coverage does not include most of the services that are offered by Medicare. However, the facility must provide all the services required at no extra charge to the resident under Medicaid coverage. As can be seen, the government reimbursement rate is much lower than what the market can bear in the private sector. As such, nursing homes try to limit the number of beds reserved for Medicaid residents, saving the remaining beds for the more profitable private-pay residents.

A Medicaid resident with no other resources is also subject to many regulations in a certified nursing home. Many of the necessities for these residents must have prior authorization. Items such as hearing aids, dentures and medications all have restrictions attached. Sometimes specific medication ordered by a physician will not be covered by Medicaid. The nurse on duty will then have to consult with the pharmacist and place a call to the physician to see if a substitute medication that is covered by Medicaid can be used. All Medicaid residents' medications and treatment supplies must follow the Medicaid drug formulary guidelines. Some skilled nursing facilities have a copy of the state Medicaid drug formulary on hand for reference. This is where the licensed nurses can become residents' advocates. If they feel that a resident requires skilled nursing care or rehabilitation services in order to recover, they can contact the facility's Social Service Director for the purpose of making a call to the state to obtain a prior authorization number to perform the reasonable, necessary and practical care. Medicaid will cover some of the remaining balance if Medicare funds are exhausted or if the resident cannot participate in cost-sharing needed for Medicare coverage. Due to the bureaucracy associated with Medicaid distribution of funds, both physicians and facilities are often reluctant to care for these individuals. It is very difficult to find a physician and an available bed for an individual who can only qualify for Medicaid or who is on a Medicaid pending status.

PRIVATE INSURANCE:
The private-pay residents must pay monthly charges incurred for all the services provided to him/her from

his/her own funds first and then collect afterwards through his/her insurance carrier. Upon admission the resident must pay for the prorated fees for the remainder of that month and for the entire amount of the following month up front. The fees charged by the facility are set by its own guidelines. After his/her discharge from the hospital the private-pay resident certainly will have no problem being admitted to a skilled nursing facility or finding a physician to care for him/her. The professional licensed personnel of the skilled nursing facility must call his/her insurance carrier to obtain prior authorization approval before any rehabilitation services can be started.

The elderly population is often the target of many aggressive sales campaigns for supplemental long-term care insurance. How many people would not want some type of coverage that would protect their assets and at the same time, give them the ability to pay for long-term care needs? The number of companies selling long-term care policies is growing rapidly, and the benefits vary greatly. At the present time private insurance policies have not afforded the senior citizens much protection against the cost of nursing home care. Thus far, private insurance payments total less than one percent of the total nursing home costs.[29] Furthermore, currently there are no regulations which outline the type of benefits that must be offered.

In general, there are three types of long-term care policies, all designed to take effect when the Medicare coverage ceases. They are the straight insurance policy, usually designated for either nursing home use or for comprehensive long-term care assistance, the "accelerated death or living benefit rider" on life insurance, and the annuity plan that can be tapped for long-term care needs. Due to the inevitability of the need of this fund, insurance companies often attach a very high premium to these

---

[29]Lang, Daphne M., "Dollars & Sense. Comptalk", *Senior Magazine - The Capitol City Edition*, Feb. 1994, p.16.

policies. Each company sets its own guidelines. It is imperative to examine the policy carefully. Make sure you read all the fine print and understand under what conditions are nursing home benefits offered. It would definitely be worthwhile to consult your accountant, tax lawyer or financial planner before purchasing any of these policies.

How about benefits tied to a retirement or pension plan? A number of insurance companies have adopted the same federal government's Medicare guidelines with respect to total coverage, which has a very limited time frame.

Partnership Insurance in Long-Term Care:[30]

The State of California has initiated a new program designed to make the most objectionable aspect of the Medicaid program bearable for middle-class residents. It was mentioned in the section on Medicaid coverage that being eligible for such insurance requires that the individual be devoid of all assets except for $2,000, besides a home and an automobile. The new program, which is called The California Partnership for Long-Term Care is a joint venture between former assemblyman Lloyd Connelly, the Robert Wood Johnson Foundation, Governor Pete Wilson's administration, and several participating insurance companies who are offering the policies. This program is designed to alleviate the need for participants to have to spend down their assets until the $1,500 poverty level is reached. Under this program an individual can choose how much of his/her assets he/she would like to protect against the spend down in order to qualify for Medi-Cal (California version of Medicaid) insurance. For example, assume your loved one has an asset of $200,000. He/she wants to be assured that this asset will not be used, even if he/she were to go onto Medi-Cal. He/she would have to buy from private, participating insurance companies a Partnership

[30]California Department of Aging, Questions and Answers on the California Partnership for Long-Term Care, CDA-HICAP publication

Plan that entitles him/her to protect $40,000 per year for five years. Once it has been decided that he/she needs custodial care in a nursing home, the insurance company will start payment up to the value of his/her policy. When the policy is spent, he/she will only need to spend down his/her own assets to the level of insurance, that is, $200,000, before Medi-Cal begins to pick up the cost of his/her custodial care.

This program is not for the poor, nor is it for the rich. It is not for those people who are already disabled. It is specifically set up for middle-class Californians who are active and healthy. The target population is between the ages of 55 through 64, and ages 65 through 74 with Medi-Cal assets of $50,000 through $200,000. Policies can be purchased by children of these adults. Only policies approved by the partnership will include the guarantee of "Medi-Cal asset protection." Full information about this program is available by calling (800) 434-0222.

This program contains the following features:
1. Premium is age rated and once the policy is bought, it will not increase just because you get older.
2. It is for anyone who is a California resident in good general health, has   at least $30,000 in personal assets, not including a house, furniture   or a car.
3. It has an automatic guarantee against inflation.
4. Policies are written within stringent insurance standards.
5. All insurance agents must successfully go through two training sessions   before they can sell the policies:
    a. a course authorized by the State of California Insurance
       Department.
    b. a course authorized by the California Partnership for
       Long-Term Care.
6. Protection of assets equivalent to the insured individual's
       partnership policy for long-term care services.
7. The individual has the right to purchase protection equal to the amount   of assets he/she wants to protect.

There are seven insurance carriers who are offering the partnership policy for California residents. They are:

1. Amex Life Assurance
2. Bankers Life and Casualty
3. Continental Casualty (CNA)
4. John Hancock Mutual Life
5. New York Life
6. TIME Insurance
7. Transamerica Occidental Life

This program had its start in 1993 and will be reviewed in 1998. The state of California has made a commitment to honor the lifetime status of this partnership contract for those who have purchased them, irrespective of the outcome of the program evaluation. For those who are contemplating joining this plan, it is advisable that you do not cancel any of your existing insurance policies. Participating companies should offer you the chance to upgrade your policy to a Partnership policy. For others in the State of California, be sure to read, understand and compare this thoroughly with your other insurance policies before making the final decision to buy or not to buy. For residents in other states, you can start lobbying your legislature for some form of action similar to the California Partnership for Long-Term Care concept.

The traumatic activities of choosing, being admitted, and deciding on how to finance the stay in a nursing home have now been dealt with. The next four chapters will focus on the life of residents in nursing homes.

CHAPTER 7

Quality of Life

Dignity...98
Self-Determination...99
Participation in Resident and Family Groups....................107
Accommodation of Needs..110

Every resident who enters a skilled nursing facility is automatically guaranteed certain rights under state and federal laws. In the Admission chapter, you will recall that you had to read and sign papers including one that is called the "Resident Rights" and another titled the "Statutory Bill of Rights". Life in the microcosm of a society such as a nursing home depends on these rights being upheld. Being a special type of social entity, the nursing home is concerned not only with the **quality of life** of its residents, but the **quality of care** given to the residents. This chapter will concentrate on the quality of life, while the topic of quality of care will be discussed in the next chapter. Here, insights into the meaning of those resident's rights that can lead to quality of life will be given. (The boldface letters are the guaranteed rights of the residents as specified by the OBRA regulations.) This knowledge will help you and your loved one in exercising these rights and in making sure that the facility staff never violate them.

Achieving a high quality of life during one's existence is essential to a person's survival instinct and for his/her striving for independence and self-esteem. Without such a goal a person will lose the meaning of the purpose for life and slowly wither away. Translated to the nursing home environment, it is important to continue to motivate the residents so that they, in their twilight years, still have a purpose for living. The Omnibus Budget Reconciliation Act (OBRA) of 1987 gives residents the authority and the autonomy over choices and decisions. It is meant to enable the residents to exercise control over their lives, on the basis of their own unique needs, preferences, and goals. It encourages the staff to acknowledge the resident's potential for self-determination. OBRA also requires the direct and continuous involvement on the part of the residents, the administration of nursing facilities, the primary physician, the staff, and the family members of the residents. To achieve and maintain the highest level of quality of life of each individual resident should be the focusing point of the facility. In order to achieve that, we must consider several factors:

I. DIGNITY:

A. The facility must promote care for residents in a manner that maintains or enhances each resident's dignity and respect in full recognition of his/her individuality.

This means that in the facility's interactions with residents, the staff must help to carry out activities that assist the resident to maintain and enhance his/her self-worth. In the category of preserving the dignity of the resident, this is the set of rights:

1. The resident has the right to request that the staff comb his/her hair, shave or trim his/her beard, and clip or clean his/her nails the way he/she wants.

2. The staff can assist the resident in choosing what clothing to wear for the appropriate time of the day. However, the staff should not dictate these choices.

3. The resident has the right to have a quiet, odor-free, and home-like dining room environment during meal time.

4. The staff must respect a resident's private space and property, including not changing radio or television stations without prior approval of the resident.

5. Staff members must respect the resident's venerable status. They must focus their attention on the resident as an individual when the resident is speaking to them. They must listen respectfully and carefully, and address him/her with the name and title of his/her choice. The staff shall not use child-like titles on the residents and must never talk to a resident as if he/she were a child.

You can observe the staff and your loved one's interactions during your visits to see if dignity is being maintained. Do the staff show respect to your loved one? Do the staff pay attention to your loved one as an individual? Do the staff spend enough time with your loved one? How is your loved one's appearance? Is he/she neat and well groomed or unattended and uncared for? Is there an unpleasant odor about your loved one? Are his/her clothes clean, in good condition and appropriate for the time of the day?

B. The resident has the right to be informed of all the rules, regulations, conduct and responsibilities in a language that he/she understands both verbally and in writing.

If your loved one only speaks and understands his/her non-English native language (for instance, Spanish), request a copy of the rights in that language. If the native language of your loved one is some other language besides Spanish, the facility must work with one of your family members who can understand and speak English, and then have that individual in turn translate the rights to your loved one. Currently these rights have been translated into several other foreign languages (Chinese, Vietnamese, etc.). Do not let the facility tell you that they have no other foreign language rights or that they have no time to work with you. This is your right and their responsibility.

II. SELF-DETERMINATION AND PARTICIPATION:
A. The resident has the right to choose activities, schedule, and health care consistent with his/her interests,

assessment, and plan of care. He/she has the right to be able to communicate with anyone inside or outside the facility. He/she has the right to make choices about aspects of his/ her life in the facility that are significant to him/herself.

Residents have autonomy this implies they can determine how they wish to live their everyday lives and receive care, as long as they do not violate facility rules or regulations. Autonomy must be seen on an individual basis, with no set standards or criteria. Residents should be free to take control in making decisions and choices and becoming as physically independent as possible. When conditions are such that free choice is allowed, autonomy then becomes authentic both in personality and in character. Often in an institutionalized setting, autonomy or self-determination becomes subjugated to other goals for expediency purposes. As your loved one starts to live within this facility, you should take note at what expense his/her autonomy is being relinquished. You should be vocal in expecting the staff to honor the allowed level of self-determination. You should also be supportive of the staff member who is not afraid of favoring self-determination over expediency.

Example #1. A female resident was admitted to an acute hospital to re-regulate her respiratory inhalation medication regimen. Upon discharge from the hospital, she was transferred to the skilled nursing facility with a diagnosis of asthma, emphysema, and chronic obstructive pulmonary disease (COPD). Since she is alert and oriented to person, place and time, she requested to be allowed to give herself her own respiratory medications. She promised not to abuse this privilege, stating that she has already learned a lesson. Permission was granted by the physician and the nurses only needed to monitor her. At first she followed the prescribed medication schedule without any problems, which was every four hours. But slowly she reverted to her old way of increasing the dosage and shortening the intervals. The interdisciplinary team then reviewed her actions and denied further requests of self-medication with the approval of the physician.

In this example, self-administration of medication is shown to be detrimental to the health of this individual. Self-determination privilege in this area had to be revoked.

If the resident has communication, hearing or mental impairment, he/she can still exercise these rights with respect to his/her own autonomy and choices. The facility should have a pertinent picture book describing the various "activities of daily living" needs of a person. By pointing out pictures of his/her specific needs, a resident will be more comfortable in communicating with the staff.

Example #2: A Russian lady who spoke only Russian, informed her family that she did not want anything done to her if she stopped breathing or her heart stopped beating. A "CPR or no CPR" card was shown to her to make sure she understood the differences. According to her wishes, an "intensity of care" form with "No CPR" was placed in her chart. During the annual facility inspection, an inspector decided to orally interview the resident and her family members on this matter. The interviewer got the resident and the family member so confused and afraid that the Administrator and the Social Service Director had to step in to resolve the misunderstanding caused by the inspector. In the end the resident's wish of not having CPR was upheld.

In this case, autonomy and self-determination were upheld and respected. Even though the right to self-determination is sometimes fraught with confusion and uncertainty, when all points are fully clear to a resident, he/she should be allowed to exercise that right.

Example #3: A male resident who is awake, alert and oriented to person, place and time had both regained his capability to walk and improved on his breathing problem, for which he was using oxygen therapy intermittently. He was performing his own activities of daily living. He went out with his friend frequently. This act made him eligible to go to a lower level of care. He was informed both verbally and in writing that he had to move for those reasons. The Social Service Director gave him the name of a "board and care" facility to visit. After returning from the visit, he became ill and required antibiotic treatment and continuous oxygen inhalation therapy. The transfer/discharge process was stopped, and the resident remained in the facility gradually improving to his previous level. This went back and forth for several times. Finally the interdisciplinary team and the physician asked the resident if he could explain this behavior. They found out that he had become attached to the staff and considered this to be his home and his extended family. He said, "You were throwing me out to the wolves." After several discussions, the team and the Administrator agreed to let the resident remain in the facility indefinitely.

This example is a case where exercising the right of self-determination is not even explicit. This resident was psychologically rebelling against a transfer, but not voicing it openly. It shows that some significant effort has to be expended by a dedicated staff so as to not infringe upon the autonomy of this resident. The end result fortunately is a happy one. On the other hand, there could be situations where a resident really does not belong in a facility because of some overt act that infringes upon the rights of other residents and the staff.

Example #4. A male resident was admitted from his home. When he exhibited inappropriate behavior toward female residents, several types of intervention were attempted. A psychiatrist was called upon to treat this resident to no avail. His behavior worsened. The Administrator, the nursing department, the social service department and the State Ombudsman worked together to discharge the resident to a more appropriate facility. In this case, the nursing department and the Social Service Director also worked very closely with the resident's wife and his son to keep them informed of the situation. The facility has the responsibility to protect other residents when their collective safety is endangered. A verbal notice shall be given first, to be followed with a written notice indicating the seriousness and urgency of the situation.

Example #5. A male resident who was in his early forties, did not want to be admitted to the facility. However, he was too weak to go home without extra help. He had to sign himself in, but he continued to fight with the staff and other residents in the facility by verbally abusing and accusing them without any provocation. Since he signed himself into the facility, verbal notice and a follow-up written letter were given directly to him for the discharge within thirty days.

Another aspect of daily living that is very significant to a particular resident is the rigid daily schedule of activities. The following are the statements made by several residents of a convalescent home, as reported by Carter Catlett Williams:[31]

"I'd rather not get up so early every morning and sit in my wheelchair and wait more than an hour for breakfast. I'd really like to get up about 7:30 the way I did at home instead of between 5:30 and 6:00 AM as I have to do now. "

This is a classical case of individual wishes vs. institutional rules. It is true that the CNAs are on a tight schedule to get all the residents prepared for the day within a certain amount of time. However, there can be a solution to this problem: The facility should allow certain flexibility for the night CNAs to get residents who request to be up early first, and leave the rest until the AM shift arrives to assist in finishing the task. You should present your loved one's request to the Nursing Supervisor, the Charge Nurse, or the Director of Nursing. They can then compile a list of residents who would like to get up a little earlier or later.

---

[31]Williams, Carter Catlett, Long-Term Care and the Human Spirit, *Generations*, Fall, 1990, p26. (Reprinted with permission from Generations, 833 Market Street, Suite 511, San Francisco, CA 94103. Copyright 1990, ASA).

"When I was told (by my CNA) I didn't need the bedpan because I used it only an hour ago, I was left to have the bowel movement in my bed. That broke my spirit."

The regulation states that each resident shall show evidence of good personal hygiene, be given care to prevent bedsores, and the staff shall use measures to prevent and reduce incontinence. This means that the CNA is required to take your loved one to the bathroom or to have a bedpan available at all times upon his/her request, even if he/she had just had an occasion to use it a short while ago. If your loved one tells you about an incident like the one described above, be sure to report it to the Administrator or the Director of Nursing immediately.

"May I please take my nap now? A frind came to visit me during my usual nap time." The nurse's aide replied no, because everybody must be up before the afternoon shift arrives.

Here the CNA responsible for that resident has confused her time constraint with stated regulations. There are no rules in any facility to say that everybody must be up before the PM shift arrives, even if it is a practice of convenience. If your loved one tells you about this be sure to let the nursing supervisor know. The nursing department should be able to put all the residents who request to have an afternoon nap on a special list and have the PM shift staff get them up before dinner.

"That paper taped to my mirror is the schedule for when I'll be taken to the bathroom.... they brought it to me." without any inputs from the resident.

In this case, this type of schedule speaks for the fact that in this facility the accomplishment of a task within a prescribed time interval takes precedence over the needs of the individual resident. These are convenience guidelines for the nursing staff, and they should have involved inputs of the resident.

"The dining room is a madhouse, I hate to go to meals --- there's so much noise and so many bad odors......"

Common dining halls will always have some of these complaints. In a nursing home, it is possible to minimize the frequency of these complaints by the following simple procedure: Propose to the DON to have nursing assistants take residents to the bathroom before eating. For others who are incontinent, put diapers on them before they are sent to the dining hall. This will guard against accidents and odors. There should always be a licensed nurse in the dining room to monitor the environment during each meal. In the event of any inadvertent commotion or emergency, the licensed nurse can take charge.

"I am sorry Mrs. R--- I have to tie you to your chair with this vest restraint to be sure you don't fall and break a bone," a CNA says to the resident.

This topic will be discussed in a later chapter thoroughly by itself. It is a legal requirement that there must be a physician's order and a specific reason for the use of any physical restraint. A consent form must also have been signed by the resident and his/her family before such action can be taken. This action taken unilaterally by the CNA is against the law.

B. Right of citizenship - voting

A resident should be able to exercise the right and privilege to vote at the important elections. The Activities Director can and should obtain absentee ballots for any resident who wants to vote, and she should make sure that there are simple instructions so that the resident can understand what to do. However, the family members should be made aware that sometimes exercising this right may be unfeasible for their loved one due to mental impairment.

C. The resident has the right to choose his/her own personal attending physician

The facility should be able to provide the resident with the name, the specialty, and the method of contacting his/her own physician who is responsible for his/her care. Sometimes this right is very hard to comply with because of many built-in constraints. As we had mentioned in the previous chapters, if your loved one is a private paying individual with good medical coverage, there are no problems. If you are on a strictly Medicaid insurance, the choice is limited. Physicians are free to accept or deny Medicaid residents. Often as a last resort, the responsibility falls on the shoulder of the facility's Medical Director, who will be the one to assume the care. Often times, residents do not even know they have this right of physician selection.

D. A resident has the right to be fully informed in advance about participating in planning care and treatment. He/she has the right to refuse treatment, changes in treatments, or treatments that may affect his/her well-being. He/she also has the right to refuse to participate in experimental research, and to formulate advance directives if he/she is not incapacitated or incompetent.

Example: A resident required physical therapy to learn to walk again after she broke her hip. She refused the treatment ordered by the physician. Each time the physical therapist wanted her to walk, she became verbally abusive and combative toward this individual. The Social Service Director was asked to find out the reason for the refusal. In this case, the resident said, "I have pain when I walk, and I do not like her (the PT)." With this information the nursing staff contacted the physician and obtained the order for pain control. The Physical Therapy Department was contacted to change the therapist. During her next scheduled session, the medication nurse gave her the pain pill thirty minutes before the therapy. When she experienced no pain she started to increase her ambulating distances daily. At the end of three weeks she was discharged for home.

In the above example, it has been pointed out that whenever a resident complains or refuses to do his/her therapy, it is up to the licensed staff to determine exactly why the resident is refusing the treatment? The licensed staff must also clarify and educate the resident, as to the consequences of refusal. An offer of alternative treatment should be included if possible. This is where you can help the facility staff convince your loved one how important these treatments are and to comply with the physician's orders.

E. The resident has the right to refuse to perform services for the facility.

If any resident decides to work for the facility, whether on a voluntary basis or for pay, it must be documented in the care plan. He/she must be paid according to the going rate in the community.

III. PARTICIPATION IN RESIDENT AND FAMILY GROUPS :

Each new resident brings with him/her his/her own personality and preferences. Even though the nursing home surrounding limits what types of activities and hobbies can be pursued, the facility, through its Activities Director, should anticipate and provide for a wide enough range of activity programs so that a maximum number of residents can and will want to participate in them.

A. Resident Council:

The facility must allow residents to form their own council, and elect their own officers to discuss any pertinent problems and needs of the residents within the facility. Staff members are not allowed to attend without implicit invitation from the council. The facility must provide a private space for group meetings and a staff person to assist and follow up with the group's requests. This person is usually the Activity Director. Minutes of the meeting are passed on to the appropriate department heads.

B. Family council:

Usually the residents and family members do not verbalize their opinions or complaints to the Administration as to whether they are pleased or displeased with the care. Residents also feel that staff are too busy during their shift, for them to bother the nurses and voice their concerns. Many residents and their family members also fear retaliation if they complain, but the facility must listen to and act upon requests or concerns of the residents and the group. Individual resident families have the right to visit with other families in the facility.

The best way to voice and hopefully resolve problems and concerns is to attend the family council meeting, usually held once each month. The staff members who are present are the Administrator, various Department Heads, and the Nursing Director and/or Supervisors. This is the time and place to voice your legitimate complaints, and frustration, offer various viewpoints, and obtain information and suggestions. The staff will respond if families show they care about the facility. Do not take the excuse, "We are short of help." After the meeting, if you still feel that proper attention has not been given to a specific problem, ask questions. Speak with the Administrator, the Director of Nursing, the social worker or the therapists. Do not shout at, argue with, or try to intimidate the staff. Talk it out in a cooperative and friendly manner. If you still are not satisfied with their response, you can contact the State Ombudsman assigned to that facility. Finally you can also contact the State Licensing and Certification Department to issue your concerns. You do not have to give your name in this report.

If you are particularly pleased with an employee and want to praise this single staff person, take down and then give that name of the staff member to the Administration with a note of praise. The Administration can notify this particular individual and put the letter of praise in the employee file.

C. Visits and visitors:

The facility must provide the residents with immediate access to any of these individuals without any restriction regarding the visiting hours limitations. These include:

   a. Any representative of the Secretary of State.
   b. Any representative of the State.
   c. The resident's individual physician.
   d. The State long-term care Ombudsman.
   e. The agency responsible for the protection and advocacy system for developmentally disabled and mentally ill individuals.

Family members are not subject to visiting hour limitations or other restrictions not imposed by the resident. All other individuals have the right of reasonable access to the resident. In most facilities, the visiting hours are between 10 A.M. and 9 P.M.. A resident has the right to refuse to see any of the above individuals. He/she can also request to have a facility staff member stay with him/her during their time of contact. The facility has the right to change the location of visits in order to assist the staff and to protect the privacy of other residents.

D. The resident has the right to choose activities, schedules and health care consistent with his/her or her interests.

The facility must be equipped to meet the needs and interests of each resident by providing activities that encourage self care and resumption of normal activities. Residents shall be encouraged to participate in activities suited to their individual needs.

For sensory stimulation the facility's Activities Director may use water fountains, goldfish, colorful artwork, low mirror, percolator coffee, animals, music (old and modern), hot-roll baking, popcorn popping, ice cream making, specialty craft rooms (sewing, crocheting, knitting, embroidery), an up-to-date library, bingo games, other art and crafts, and woodworking equipment and supplies. For ladies, putting on rouge, powder, lipstick and nail polish can also become activities to provide further sensory stimulation.

IV. ACCOMMODATION OF NEEDS:

The facility must have a conducive environment and staff behavior to assist residents in maintaining independent functioning, dignity, well-being and self-determination. These individual needs and preferences are as follows:

A. The resident has the right to authorize the facility to manage his/her funds.

PRIVATE FUNDS:

1. The facility must deposit any resident's personal funds in excess of $50 in an interest bearing account. The business office manager must give resident's monthly bank notice.

2. The facility must maintain a resident's personal fund that does not exceed $50 in a non-interest-bearing account or a petty-cash fund for his/her personal use. This money is usually kept with the business office manager in a double locked container/drawer. The Administrator and sometimes the Director of Nursing may also have the key in case of an emergency.

3. The facility may not impose a charge against the personal funds of a resident for any items or services for which payment is made under Medicaid or Medicare.

4. In the event of the death of a resident with a personal fund deposited with the facility, the facility must have a final accounting of those funds and return all the unspent funds within thirty days to the individual's responsible party or probate court.

NOTICE OF CERTAIN ENTITLEMENT BALANCES:

Besides the private account, the facility must also keep a running balance of an individual resident's entitlement account. Primarily, these entitlements are the Medicaid and the Social Security Insurance (SSI) benefits.

The facility must notify each resident who receives Medicaid benefits when the SSI resource limit for that individual is about to be reached. It is at this limit that the resident may lose eligibility for Medicaid or SSI. An individual cannot have both the SSI and the Medicaid insurance when he/she enters a SNF. Instead, he/she must apply for Long-Term Care Medicaid. By doing that, the SSI coverage is dropped.

The facility must inform each resident who is entitled to Medicaid benefits, in writing, at the time of admission to the nursing facility, or when the resident becomes eligible for Medicaid, all of the following:

1. The items and services that are included in nursing facility services under the state plan, and for which the resident may not be charged.

2. Services available in the facility and of charges for those services, including any charges for services not covered under Medicare or by the facility's per diem rate.

B. The resident has the right to privacy in written communication including the right to send and promptly receive mail that is unopened. He/she shall have access to writing materials and postage stamps in the business office, but these will be provided at the resident's own expense.

The only mail the business office manager opens are the residents' monthly Social Security checks and the Medicaid stickers. The Social Service Director or the business manager will take the check to the resident for his/her signature.

C. The resident has the right to have reasonable access to the use of a telephone where calls can be made without being overheard by others.

All facilities must have phones at a height for wheelchair-bound residents and have phones especially adapted for use by the hearing impaired. You can make arrangements to install a private telephone in your loved one's room, provided you foot the bill. Each month, check your telephone bill before paying it. If you find there is a discrepancy, bring the bill to the business office and have the facility straighten it out for you. Once in a great while there may be some staff member who will abuse this right of the resident. The facility's Social Service Director will investigate this matter and find the culprit. There are also ways that the telephone company can help you safeguard your loved one's private phone use. Call them to find out how.

D. The resident has the right to retain and use personal possessions, including appropriate clothing and some furnishings as space permit, unless to do so would infringe upon the rights, health and safety of his/her roommate.

Any electrical equipment must have three prongs to prevent a fire hazard. You must also get prior approval from the Administrator or the maintenance supervisor to use this equipment. All residents must protect the facility's property for future residents' use. Your loved one can bring small armchairs, pictures, a radio, a television, and his/her own bedding to use if he/she desires. Please mark all of these personal belongings first. Make sure that all new clothing you bring in to the resident are listed in the resident's clothing list. They should all be marked with your loved one's name. These inventory lists are located in each individual resident's chart. The nursing staff, the Activities Director, and the Social Service Director can all help you with this task whenever the need arises.

An example: A male resident's family members complained about their father's personal clothes, glasses, and dentures getting lost. They complained that each time they brought in a new set of clothing, it was either "lost", or on somebody else. The glasses and dentures were never on their father's face or in his mouth. They made numerous complaints to the previous Administration without getting any results. Consequently the family members took legal action against the facility. When the new Administration was notified of these problems, it responded by holding a meeting with the responsible family member. An investigation was conducted. It was discovered that this resident is mildly confused and disoriented. He likes to put his dentures in his sleeves, near his hips, or wrap them in napkins and place them at different locations. Furthermore, none of his clothing had been marked with names. The staff suggested that personal items be marked and reported to the office for inventory listing. Since he roams the facility in his wheelchair, the staff obtained a chain for his glasses, used more denture paste for his dentures, and watched him closely. The Social Service Director also informed the family that the washing machine's temperature is very high, and it shrank the wool shirts, sweaters and even sweat suits to the point that the resident could not wear them anymore. They were therefore either discarded or donated to others who can better fit them. In addition, the facility immediately replaced some of the lost or shrunken items and gave money to replace other items. A legal nightmare was thus avoided.

E. Social services:

The facility must provide medically-related social services to attain or maintain the highest practical physical, mental, and psycho-social well-being of each resident. If a resident displays mental or psychosocial adjustment difficulty, decreased social interaction/ increased withdrawal, anger, or depressive behavior, he/she must receive appropriate treatment and services to correct the problem.

F. Smoking guidelines:

For both health and safety reasons, no resident is allowed to smoke in his/her room. If the facility has recently converted to a "no-smoking" facility, it must allow current residents who have been smoking in the facility to continue to smoke in a designated smoking area. All private cigarettes and lighters must be kept at the nurses' station or with the Activity Director and passed out at a specific time, usually every four hours. Most facilities have assigned smoking hours through AM and PM shifts. One of the CNAs who smokes will sit with the residents to supervise smoking either in the designated area or outside on the patio so they will not injure themselves. This is to prevent fire hazards. The Activity Director is also the person responsible for buying the cigarettes.

An example: Two ladies and a gentleman would go to the business office every Friday and request cash to buy the cigarettes for next week's supply. They also go to the Nurses' Station every four hours to ask for cigarettes. Since they are both alert, oriented and responsible, the staff will light up for them, then they immediately go out to the designated area or the patio to smoke. As a show of their responsible nature, they received permission to assign themselves as "police officers" to monitor other smoking residents during smoking hours. They relish this duty immensely. Of course, another staff is present also.

G. Theft and losses

The cases of overt theft that were reported in the "20/20" program[32] certainly do occur in isolated incidence. Fortunately, in my experience, that is far from the norm in the typical facility where references of employees are subject to even the most cursory checks. More than likely, reported theft and losses are the result of less flagrant actions. Residents who are not alert or oriented sometimes will wander around and collect things that do not belong to them. Sometimes the facility is at fault if a staff member puts

[32]Crier, Catherine, in a segment of the "20/20" program, ABC Network, January 13, 1995.

an individual resident's clothes into another resident's closet. It is also conceivable that during their busy schedule in the morning, a CNA might grab clothes and socks from a closet without carefully reading the name and put them on the wrong resident. At other times the staff member may have a difficult time distinguishing various colors herself. For the majority of time, personal belongings are usually found.

If you loved one loses belongings that cost $25.00 or more, go to the Social Services Director and fill out a form. She will initiate an investigation. If the facility is at fault for the items lost, the facility will have to either replace them or give you cash value so that you can purchase the replacement yourself. If your loved one loses an item or items valued at less than $25.00, also let the Social Service Director know. If the facility has genuine concern for the welfare of the residents, the item will be replaced. Most of the time family members will decide such small items are not worth the trouble of reporting and filling out a form.

There was a facility where I worked that had an alarmingly high theft rate. The Administrator worked closely with the local police department to catch the responsible person; the problem was thus resolved.

H. Laundry services:

The facility is required by law to provide clean linen and bedding for all residents, no matter how many times they need to be changed daily. For personal laundry services, you should find out how much the facility will charge monthly? By using its service, the facility shall not be responsible for normal deterioration of clothing caused by routine washing. You can, on the other hand, do the laundry yourself, but you have to provide a tightly covered plastic container for soiled clothes marked with the resident's name. It must be taken home preferably every day and returned to the facility promptly. If you choose this route but fail to meet your obligations, then the facility will take the soiled clothes, wash and dry them, and charge the resident accordingly.

I. Environment:

This is the "home away from the old sweet home" that your loved one will come to know. Therefore the quality of the environment shall be clean, safe, comfortable, sanitary, in good repair and as home-like as possible. The facility must provide the resident with private closet space. To ensure that a resident has two baths a week, there is a bath schedule in the nurses station. If your loved one did not have one on his/her specific day, be sure to ask "why". If your loved one's bath schedule does not fit his/her preference, request to have the schedule changed. Each resident must have clean bed linen, changed at least twice a week, and sooner if there is a need. The facility must ensure that each resident has adequate and comfortable lighting, temperature and sound level. The room temperature is usually maintained between 72 and 82 degrees Fahrenheit all the time. This environment should not be any different from his/her own home. All facilities must provide housekeeping and maintenance services. However, some small facilities have housekeeping and maintenance services only during the day, and not on either PM or night shifts. In those situations, the Nursing Department again takes over their duties to keep the facility clean and odor-free.

All of these rights that have been discussed in this chapter are considered necessary in order that a resident can have a level of "quality of living" that he/she is accustomed to outside a facility. These rights make the transition from a life one has been used to for many years to such an institutional living condition easier. What sets this institution apart from others is the nursing care that it provides to its residents. Assuring a high level of quality of care is the topic of the next three chapters.

CHAPTER 8

Quality of Care

Activities of Daily Living 118
Vision and Hearing 121
Pressure Ulcers 121
Urinary Incontinence 123
NG and GT Tubes 124
Nutrition and Hydration 126
Change of condition 128
Routine Medications 131

This chapter and the following two chapters deal with areas that usually are cited for having most of the rule violations in nursing homes. Most of the horror stories of residents being neglected and abused are due to a lack of quality of care. The goal of eliminating the horror and fear associated with nursing home care is the basis of the new federal OBRA regulations. In a previous chapter (Chapter 2), the basic tools that new OBRA regulations carry to safeguard your loved one's well-being have already been introduced. In this chapter, precisely how that tool, the MINIMUM DATA SET or MDS, should be utilized to the fullest extent by the staff of the facilities to ensure quality of care for each of the residents will be discussed. The MDS, the Resident Assessment Protocol (RAP) and the individualized Care Plan are also the primary focus of state inspectors when they make their annual visits to facilities for recertification. The following are all the rights of the residents related to quality of care. (The boldface letters represents rights of the residents specified by the OBRA regulations.) The facilities must comply with them or face major citations, fines and/or license suspension or decertification.

ACTIVITIES OF DAILY LIVING (ADL):

The facility must ensure that the resident's abilities in activities of daily living (ADL) do not diminish unless circumstances of the individual's clinical condition demonstrate that it was unavoidable.

The facility must ensure that a resident who is unable to carry out activities of daily living will receive the necessary services to maintain good nutrition, grooming, and personal and oral hygiene.

This includes the resident's ability to eat, bathe, dress, groom, transfer, ambulate, and use the toilet. If your loved one can do these ADL independently, he has the right to do them without being hurried. If he requires partial help or is totally dependent, he has the right to receive the necessary assistance. As simple as these two guidelines are, this is an area, nonetheless, where many of the abuses, carelessness, and acts of neglect occur. To a resident, the manner in which tasks are performed means a lot. From an article by Carter C. Williams, one resident is quoted as saying, "I would like most of all to start my day without fear. I never know who will come in to help me in the morning. If I do not understand what the person wants me to do and do not move quickly enough she gets mad, fusses at me, and stomps out of the room."[33]

Most of the facilities are aware of these type of problems. A sense of the staff's knowing the resident as a person is very important. to develop a sense of familiarity, security, and continuity of care. DONs are always trying to assign the same CNA to the same residents every month unless the resident or the CNA requests a change. This gives both of them a sense of understanding where each other is coming from, and that in turn improves the quality of care.

---

[33]Williams, C. Catlett, cf. footnote 31.

Usually a very strong rapport is established between them. The residents can tell you who is a good CNA and who is not a good CNA.

Additionally, peer pressure is a good motivator for improving the quality of care. When the regular CNA returns from her days off and sees his/her group of residents had lacked quality care, he/she can and often does exert pressure on the relief personnel to "carry the load".

To guard a frail resident against infections, it is expected of the attending CNA that every resident must have his oral care performed at least twice a day. Dentures must be removed, soaked in an efferdent solution and then rinsed off with clear water and stored in a denture cup covered with clean water. The CNA should make sure that the urinal bottle and the bedpan are not placed next to the water pitcher, either on top of the night stand or on the overbed table. For confused and disoriented residents, these items might be mistaken for containers of drinking water. To further prevent contamination, external personal appliances such as comb and hair brush must be kept apart from the toothbrush and toothpaste. Toothbrush must be placed in a covered container.

Call-bell system:

In each resident's room there must be a call-bell attached to the bed. This is the immediate link between a resident's request for assistance and the staff's acknowledgment that help is on its way. Assured functioning of these call systems is the responsibility of the maintenance staff. Timely response to the calling signal is the responsibility of the nursing staff. Make sure the call bell is answered in a timely fashion, usually between 3 to 5 minutes. You or your loved one should never hear any staff person say, "I cannot help you because you are not my patient." Whoever hears or sees the lighted call bell outside the door must answer first. Then that staff member can go and get the responsible CNA for that resident to complete the request. Report any CNA to the Administration, charge nurse, Supervisor or the DON who makes the such a statement. Caring facility staff will tell you that all residents are every staff's responsibility. A good facility will not allow their staff to delineate residents.

An example: During an annual facility inspection, an awake, alert and oriented resident wrote a letter and handed it to the inspector, stating that a CNA was verbally and emotionally abusive to her. She cited a specific incidence in which the call-bell was taken away from her at night due to her persistent usage. She could not call the staff for help to use the bathroom or the bedpan, so she wet the bed sheet from head to toe. She had to lie on that until the day shift CNA arrived to change it for her. This is a clear case of outright physical and emotional abuse. It violates the resident's right to self-dignity and respect. The CNA's actions were investigated immediately, and appropriate action was taken by the owner/Administrator/DON.

Privacy and dignity:

Residents must be granted privacy and dignity when going to the bathroom and in other activities of personal hygiene. They should be covered completely from the neck down when they are being taken to the shower room. A shower poncho is best to use for this purpose. When a resident is being changed or given treatments in the room, the staff must close the door and/or draw curtains completely on four sides without leaving any gaps. Only authorized staff members directly involved in the care or treatment should be present. People not involved in the care should not be present without the resident's consent. When a resident is using the toilet a staff member should shut the bathroom door and stand outside to wait for the call.

All staff should knock before entering the room and should call the resident by titles such as Mr. or Mrs. So-and-so unless directed otherwise. The staff should never use a nickname, such as sweetie, honey, gramps, cutie, good girl, or that'a boy, because it shows disrespect for the person. Elderly residents should not be treated as children.

VISION AND HEARING:
To ensure that the resident receives proper treatment and assistive devices to maintain vision and hearing abilities, the facility must assist the resident in making appointments and by arranging transportation to and from the office of a practitioner, or the office of a professional specializing in vision and hearing devices. All facilities also maintain outside contracts with professional practitioners or companies who will come to the facility to do the necessary examinations for your loved one.

If your loved one needs a pair of glasses, dentures, or a hearing aid, the person within the facility to contact is the Social Service Director. You may have to pay the bill for those services if Medicare or Medicaid will not cover the cost. All facilities have contracts with an ophthmalogist, an optometrist, a dentist and an audiologist for them to visit the residents in the facility. Occasionally, the Social Service Director will arrange for a wheelchair van to and from the practitioner's office if there is such a need. You have to accompany your loved one there for safety reasons.

PRESSURE ULCERS (BEDSORES OR DECUBITUS):
The facility must ensure that a resident who enters a facility without pressure ulcers does not develop pressure ulcers unless the individual's clinical condition demonstrates that they were unavoidable.

A resident who has pressure ulcers must receive necessary treatment and services to promote healing, to prevent infection and to prevent new ulcers from developing.
The most common sites for pressure ulcers are the ears, the elbows, the shoulder blade areas, both hip areas, the buttock area, the coccyx (tail bone) area, between the knees, the heels, and the ankles. Important contributing factors to

pressure ulcers are: immobility, shear, diabetes, chronic bladder and bowel incontinence, terminal cancer and severe peripheral vascular disease. In order to prevent pressure ulcers from developing on any inactive or bedridden residents, the CNA has the responsibility to carry out prescribed measures of intervention and prevention, including the use of eggcrate mattresses, and checking the skin daily for any redness or breaks, reporting to the licensed nurse immediately if there are any. Other measures of prevention are massaging the prominent areas most likely to develop the ulcer and making sure the bed sheet is dry, tight and wrinkle free. The CNA should be using the draw sheet to lift the resident. If the resident is bedridden, he/she needs to be turned from left to right and to the back every 2 hours. If a resident is sitting, he needs to stand up and do some active or passive exercises every two hours.

The four stages of pressure sores are:

Stage I: The skin is intact, but the redness will not go away after skin massage, or when pressure is relieved for several minutes.

Stage II: Blister, abrasion or shallow crater has formed on the skin.

Stage III: A full thickness of the skin is lost; its appearance is that of a crater exposing some tissue and muscle.

Stage IV: A full thickness of skin and subcutaneous tissue are lost. The skin area of concern presents a big opening, exposing both muscle and bone. This requires surgical intervention to heal.

If there is a stage III or stage IV pressure ulcer, Medicare, private insurance and sometimes Medicaid (after obtaining prior authorization) may help pay for the necessary therapeutic bed and treatments to heal the wound. Most of the time these advanced stages of decibutus require surgical intervention. There should be a physician's order to enlist the expertise of a Physical Therapist and/or a wound specialist in the care of your loved one. They can do debridement of the wound if there are dead tissue. Without proper aggressive treatment serious consequences may occur.

URINARY INCONTINENCE:

A resident who enters the facility without an indwelling foley catheter is not catheterized unless his clinical condition shows to the contrary.

A resident who is incontinent of bladder receives appropriate treatment and services to prevent urinary tract infection and to restore as much normal bladder function as possible.

This is another culprit that will cause pressure ulcers. It is very important that a resident with incontinence be kept clean and dry. The only time an indwelling catheter can be used is when there is a valid medical reason, such as a dysfunctional bladder or when there are severe pressure ulcers on the buttock and coccyx areas. If your loved one has a Foley catheter, make sure the drainage bag is always at the foot of the bed, below the knee to allow the urine to drain downward.

If your loved one is incontinent, the CNA also has the task of monitoring and rehabilitating him in accordance with his care plan. To put a resident on a bladder retraining program requires a team effort. Physician and nurses must initially do a comprehensive assessment. The resident and his family members must be involved in the retraining program. There must be an order from the physician to put the resident on a bladder retraining program and to increase oral fluid. The Dietary Supervisor must be notified to put extra fluids on the meal tray. All shift will have in-service training on this subject. An intake and output sheet must be initiated. The resident will receive between 2,000 to 3,000 cc of fluids per day. The Rehabilitation Assistant (RA) and the CNA will take the resident to the bathroom every two hours during the day and afternoon shifts and every two to four hours at night using either the urinal or a bedpan. The retraining session will last for fourteen days, and then the program is reassessed for results.

Sometimes if a resident has fecal impaction, this may lead to incontinence due to pressure on the bladder. Make sure that your loved one has at least one bowel movement every three days. There should be a bowel check list posted at the nursing station.

RANGE OF MOTION:

The facility must ensure that a resident who enters the facility without a limited range of motion does not experience reduction in range of motion unless the resident's clinical condition demonstrates that a reduction is unavoidable.

A resident with a limited range of motion receives appropriate treatment and services to increase the range of motion and/or to prevent further decrease in range of motion.

Every resident in the facility should be on a maintenance program for mobility. This is the duty of the Restorative Aide (RA). She works under the supervision of the Physical Therapist. She does ambulation, active and passive range of motion, and sets up classes for grooming, arts and crafts.

NASOGASTRIC/GASTROSTOMY FEEDING TUBES:

The facility must ensure that a resident who has been able to eat enough alone or with a CNA's help is not fed by a nasogastric tube unless the resident's condition demonstrates that use of this is unavoidable.

A resident who is fed by nasogastric or gastrostomy tube must receive appropriate treatment and services to prevent aspiration pneumonia, diarrhea, vomiting, dehydration, metabolic abnormalities, and nasal-pharyngeal ulcers and must try to restore, if possible, normal function.

A nasogastric (NG) tube is a tube inserted into the nose through the esophagus and into the stomach. A gastrostomy (GT) tube is a tube surgically placed that passes through the skin of the abdominal wall to the stomach. This procedure is done in the operating room where a surgeon will first make a small opening through the abdominal wall and then insert the tube directly into the stomach. After placement, he will put stitches around the tube to hold it in place. This is a special type of tube and only the surgeon can change the tube. Although it is an invasive procedure, the use of the GT tube is much safer and more comfortable than the long NG tube for your loved one.

Residents who require the use of NG or GT tubes are those with severe swallowing problems such as those brought on by a stroke or other debilitating illnesses. Danger in this type of feeding is when contents from the stomach back up, causing complications such as aspirated pneumonia. In order to prevent this danger, the nursing staff must make sure the head of the bed is elevated 30 degrees at all times. If your loved one has a NG tube, make sure that the nurses check the position and placement of the tube every shift by using the stethoscope every time before feeding or passing medicine to your loved one. To prevent the tube from clogging up, nurses must flush the tube every time after its use. To prevent infection, the irrigation set and the feeding bags are changed every 24 hours. If your loved one has a GT tube, the position and placement should also be checked every shift. The site should be checked and dressing should be changed every day by the treatment nurse. If there is redness, drainage, or irritation around the site, the physician must be notified, and treatment initiated. For safer and more uniform feeding over time, a feeding pump is recommended. For residents with swallowing problems, the Speech Pathologist should evaluate the swallowing condition periodically so that the resident can be weaned off these tube feedings if feasible.

NUTRITION:

The facility shall provide food of the quality and quantity to meet the resident's needs in accordance with the doctor's orders. There must be no more than fourteen hours between a substantial evening meal and breakfast the following day.

The facility must ensure that a resident maintains acceptable parameters of nutritional status and receives a therapeutic diet when there are nutritional problems such as weight loss, heart disease, or diabetes, high blood pressure, or constipation.

Institutional food has always been the butt of many jokes ever since one entered the first public school. For the senior resident in a nursing home, this is a very great concern. The nutrient value, the caloric intake and the fluid intake of an individual resident require very careful monitoring. Adverse effects due to an inadequate diet can rapidly deteriorate a frail and elderly person's bodily functions. Furthermore, each individual has his own special needs under a physician's prescription these requirements should be adhered to strictly by the nursing and dietary staff.

To figure out how much your loved one ate, you can use this percentage chart.

Breakfast: toast=15%, entree=40%, cereal=20%, juice= 10%, and milk=15%.

Lunch and dinner: starch=20%, meat=30%, vegetable=10%, milk=15%, soup or salad=10%, dessert=10% bread and butter= 5%. If your loved one eats less than 70% of the amount on his tray, talk to the charge nurses and the Dietary Supervisor.

You can ask staff the following questions: What diet is being ordered for my loved one? If he does not like some of the items on the tray, are there any substitutes? Is the posted menu identical to the foods that are being served? Are there any licensed nurses checking the trays for the particular, correct diet before they are served to the residents? Is there an accurate monitoring of the percentage of food intake? What are the steps to take if there is a weight loss over a period of thirty days?

All diets are medically prescribed by each individual resident's own physician and must be enforced by the Dietary Department and the staff. If your loved one refuses to eat some food you can request a substitute, as long as it is within reason. Let the staff know so they can go to the kitchen to get a replacement diet. Do not eat the resident's foods yourself because the percentage of intake being counted will be inaccurate. If you bring food or beverage into the facility, also let the nursing staff know. Otherwise, unnecessary treatments, medication, or lab work may be ordered for your loved one. If you bring any cookies, candy or fruits, you must bring an air tight container to store these foods. This will keep the perishables clean and at the same time eliminate roaches and ants.

Residents who are losing weight, those who are placed on a therapeutic diet and all diabetic residents who receive insulin must have two snacks during the day and a snack before retiring. Observe to note if this is carried out by the nursing staff. For some of the residents with insomnia, a refreshment consisting of a glass of milk and some graham crackers often is satisfying. This simple procedure calms them down and eliminates the use of chemical restraints.

HYDRATION:

The facility must provide each resident with sufficient fluid intake to maintain proper hydration and health.

Signs of dehydration may be pale skin, dull eyes, red swollen lips, swollen or dry tongue with a scarlet hue, poor skin turgor (to test this, pinch a little piece of skin on back of the hand or on the stomach. If it stands up and goes down slowly, then it is a sign of dehydration), muscle wasting, calf tenderness, and reduced urine output.

To prevent urinary tract infections and constipation, and to maintain good skin tone, the staff should pass water for the residents to drink at least every 2 hours. This is where you can help the staff significantly by encouraging your loved one to drink. You can bring soft drink into the facility as a treat for your loved one if he is not on a specific, restricted fluid intake regimen or his fluid intake and output are not being monitored. Every resident has fresh water in a clean pitcher, a glass and a tray at his bedside stand everyday. CNA must change water on the day and PM shifts. During your visit check to see that the water is clean and fresh and that it is being consumed. Report any deficiencies to the Charge Nurses and/or the Nursing Supervisor. Serious complications of dehydration include fecal impaction, fever, confusion, disorientation and even death.

The staff should not tell you that the facility does not have any extra water pitchers or cups. They are usually stored in the central supply room. The charge nurse or the Nursing Supervisor always has the key to this room.

CHANGE OF CONDITION

The facility must immediately inform the resident's physician, and the responsible party when there is:

a. an accident involving the resident which results in injury and has the potential for requiring physician intervention.

b. a significant change in the resident's physical or mental status or a need to alter treatment significantly.

c. a decision to transfer or discharge the resident from the facility.

The facility must ensure that the resident's environment remains as free of accidental hazards as is possible. Each resident must receive adequate supervision and assistive devices to prevent accidents.

You can request the facility to order "long-arm" and "long-leg" protective sleeves to be put on your loved one if his skin is very thin and prone to tearing. To prevent injury from falling out of bed, the mattress can be put on the floor at night with prior approval from the Administrator.

When an accident occurs with or without injury, the licensed nurses must first assess the resident from head to toe before he is allowed to be moved. Vital signs are taken right away. The physician is notified of the incident new orders are obtained that might be needed to treat the fall. For an unobserved fall, neurological signs are checked every fifteen minutes for an hour, followed by every thirty minutes for one hour, then every hour for the first day, and finally every shift for seventy-two hours. Neurologic checks include pupil checks and hand grip checks on both sides. In this way any unusual signs/symptoms that the resident might develop will be noticed immediately, and the physician will be called in for early intervention.

You can request a thorough assessment of your loved one's medications regimen if you suspect the change of condition is due to drugs. There are numerous drug-to-drug and drug-to-food interactions. A blood test (CBC), a chemistry panel, an electrolytes test and a drug toxicity test done can be early intervention procedures.

SPECIAL NEEDS:

The facility must ensure that residents receive proper treatment and care for the following special nursing services: injections, parenteral and enteral fluids, care of a colostomy, ureterostomy, ileostomy, tracheotomy, tracheal suction, respiratory care, foot care and prostheses.

Most of these facilities will have services for injections, enteral fluids, colostomy, respiratory care, foot and prosthetic devices. Some of the facilities have established subacute units; all of the above nursing services will be provided within that unit. If your loved one needs one of these special services, be sure to find out that the facility can provide them before you make that final decision in placement. You should also ask how qualified is the staff who work in this unit when carrying out these special functions? Remember the old adage: an ounce of prevention is worth a pound of cure.

INDEPENDENT CONTRACTORS:

Every facility must have contracts with individuals or agencies to cover all potential needs of the residents for the following services: physical therapist, occupational therapist, speech therapist, podiatrist, ophthalmologist, optometrist, dentist, audiologist, social work consultant, activity consultant, dietary consultant and pharmacy consultant. Each facility also contracts to have portable x-ray machines and laboratory services performed on-site. The purpose of having these specialists on call is to use their specialties as the needs arise. Often these specialists sit on the facility's Quality Assurance Board. Periodically this board meets and reviews special problems of the facility and individual residents. They are also responsible for giving staff in-service education.

If a facility has a significant beneficial interest in an ancillary health service provider or a facility, or if a facility knows that an ancillary health provider has a significant interest in it, then the facility must disclose such interests in writing to all the residents. The facility must also advise the resident or his responsible party that they may choose to have another ancillary health service provider to provide any supplies or services ordered by a member of the medical staff of the facility.

These clauses mean that if not specified by the individual resident to the contrary, any supplies used or prescriptions to be filled will be coming from that pharmacy contracted by the facility. This procedure generally does not affect the resident's well-being, and can expedite access of needed supplies or drugs at all times of the day or night

PHARMACY:

Amongst the contracted services, pharmacy needs are those that are probably best served by allowing the facility to use its designee. Remember you do have the right to choose the use of the facility's designated pharmacy or to indicate your personal preference of a pharmacy. However, as was argued previously, using the facility's contracted one can save you headaches and time. Aside from the idea of "freedom of choice", there is no real benefit unless you or your family owns that pharmacy.

ROUTINE MEDICATIONS:

No medications can be brought to the facility from home without prior approval from the physician.

The best thing is not to bring them into a facility, because the facility cannot use them. Their presence can even delay the administration of required care to your loved one because any medication your bring into the facility must be identified by the facility's pharmacist before it can be given. Medications that are ordered by the physician will be covered under either Medicaid or Medicare. If the specific brand name of medicine is not covered, the facility's nurse will call the pharmacist to find out which comparable drug will be covered by the insurance and then call the physician to request that alternative medication.

Most of the medications are given on a routine basis. Medication for the relief of cough, pain, and diarrhea are provided if the resident asks for it. The abbreviation for that is "PRN"-whenever necessary. The administration of these PRN medications is usually explained very thoroughly by the nurse to the resident or the responsible party. You can assist the facility to reinforce and to make sure that your loved one does request these medications when he/she needs it.

MEDICATION ERRORS:

The facility must ensure that it is free of medication error at a rate of five percent or less, and the residents are free of any signs of significant medication errors.

The only way that licensed nurses will not make any drug mistakes is to follow the five "rights": **right patient, right drug, right dose, right route, right time.** All routine medications must be given within a period one hour before or one hour after the time prescribed by the physician. For instance if a drug is ordered for 9 AM, the nurse can give it between 8 AM and 10 AM, but no earlier or later. Routinely, medication pass hours are 9AM-1-5-9PM. Special medications are given according to the prescription. You can help the nurses tremendously at these times by not calling the facility or interrupting him/her during medication pass time.

INFECTION CONTROL PROGRAMS:

The facility must establish and maintain an infection control program designed to provide a safe, sanitary, and comfortable environment in order to help prevent the development and transmission of disease and infection.

Any employee with a communicable disease or infected skin lesions must be prohibited from direct contact with residents or their food. Hand washing and wearing gloves are considered a part of universal precautions. All staff must wash their hands both before and after direct contact with the resident even if they wear gloves. Other occasions the staff should wash their hands include: before handling food or food trays, after contact with contaminated objects, after blowing his/her nose, before and after using the bathroom, and after contacting soiled linen. In addition, to ensure health and safety for the residents, nurses must change oxygen equipment and humidifier bottles every five days.

As mentioned before, the goals for the facility and the staff are for the residents to attain and to maintain the highest practical function in term of physical, mental, spiritual, and psychosocial well-being. In an idealized setting when these goals are achieved, every resident will have the highest quality of life and quality of care for the remaining days of his/her life. However, non-ideal situations exist far too often, and two main culprits are the unauthorized use of chemical and physical restraints. These form the topics of the next two chapters.

CHAPTER 9

The Use of Chemical Restraints

OBRA guideline on chemical restraint.................................134
    Definition of chemical restraints 135
    Diagnoses 138
Common Psychotropic Drugs 141
    Side effects...144
    What can you do 145
Commentary: A pattern of misuse 146

One of the most significant reform measures under the OBRA regulations is the provision to protect residents from inappropriate use of chemical restraints.[34] Specifically, OBRA regulation states that **a resident has the right to be free from any chemical drugs that are imposed for the purpose of <u>discipline</u> or <u>convenience</u>, and are not required to treat the resident's specific medical symptoms.** In order to enforce this regulation, OBRA has also changed the assessment method from the medical model to a psychosocial model using the Minimum Data Set (MDS) which was discussed in Chapter 4. Using this method of assessment, each resident is assessed as a total person with distinctive individual problems. Having defined these problems, an interdisciplinary team then develops a care plan specifically tailored for that resident.

As for the use of drugs for chemical restraints, OBRA states that **the resident who has not used such drug therapy**

---

[34]<u>OBRA Making it Work: A Surveyor's Study Guide to Antipsychotic Drug Use in Nursing Homes</u>, Am. Health Care Association, 1992

before his/her admission is not to be given any of these drugs unless it is necessary to treat a <u>specific</u> condition as diagnosed and documented in the clinical record. Those residents who are placed on these drugs must have a well-developed plan for behavior modification, for drug holiday, for gradual dose reduction, and finally, for the total elimination of these drugs.

This regulation further stipulates that a resident's drug regimen must be free from <u>unnecessary</u> drugs. An unnecessary drug is any drug used 1. in excessive dose (including duplication dose), 2. for excessive duration, 3. without adequate monitoring or indications for its use, and 4. if there are any side effects. In that case, the dose should be reduced or the drug discontinued.

As the responsible person for a resident in a nursing home, you will have a very essential role on the assessment of your loved one as to whether he/she will need or not need drug therapy of this nature. In order to become better informed about the "why, when, what and how" of these chemical drugs that are used to control an individual's "inappropriate behavior", some of the basic definitions will first be introduced. These include the terms: discipline, convenience, delirium, and dementia. Secondly, a list of the common set of mental diagnoses that may or may not suggest the need for psychotropic drugs will be given. Thirdly, the types of drugs commonly considered as chemical restraints along with their potential adverse side effects will be listed. Fourthly, alternative measures can be used to treat many of the cognitive disorders will be shown. Finally, ideas of what you can do to monitor the inappropriate use of these drugs on your loved ones in a nursing home will be provided.

I. Definitions:

<u>Discipline</u>: any action taken by the facility for the sole purpose of punishing or penalizing a particular resident who exhibits "inappropriate behavior".

Convenience: any action taken by the facility to control the resident behavior or to maintain residents with a lesser amount of effort by the facility and not necessarily in the resident's best interest.

Delirium: An acute or subacute change in mental status especially common in the elderly. Common causes are hypo or hyper- glycemia, fever, dehydration, congestive heart failure, stroke, drugs, intoxication, transfer to unfamiliar surroundings, fecal impaction, urinary retention and many more causes. The biggest culprit is the drugs. These includes painkillers (codeine, demerol, morphine, and indocin), antihistamines (benadryl, vistaril, and other over-the-counter drugs), antihypertensives (clonidine, apresolinealdomet, inderal, and reserpine), heart medicines (digoxin, diuretics), hypoglycemia (insulin), chemical restraint drugs (antianxiety, antidepressant, antipsychotic, sleeping pills). The key features of this disorder include clouding of consciousness and symptoms and signs developing over a short period of time (hours to days) these symptoms fluctuate from time to time. Other characteristics of delirium include restlessness, picking at bed clothes, attempts to get out of bed, anxiety, fear, irritability, excitement, delusions, and hallucinations. This condition can be reversed when the underlying conditions have been appropriately diagnosed and treated.

If your loved one exhibits some of these symptoms suddenly, you should talk to the nurse and have physician involvement. The questions to ask are:

1. Has this onset of abnormal behavior been acute?

2. Are there physical factors such as medical illness or drugs involved to bring about the episodes?

3. Are there any psychological factors to consider such as depression?[35]

---

[35]Robert L. Kane, Ouslander G. Joseph, and Abrass B. Itamar, *Essentials of Clinical Geriatrics*, Reprinted with permission from McGraw-Hill Book Co., pp 63-66, 1984.

Dementia: a syndrome of progressive and irreversible brain dysfunction characterized predominantly by cognitive losses. The most common symptoms and signs are slow disintegration of personality and intellect due to impaired insight, diminished judgment and the loss of concern. There are four types of cognitive losses: **Amnesia** is the loss of ability to learn information, and it manifests itself as forgetfulness. **Aphasia** is difficulty in comprehending or expressing language. This may be due to a stroke or any other neurological problem. **Apraxia** is the loss of ability to perform learned motor skills, such as how to use a knife and fork, how to dress or how to use the toilet. Staff sometimes label residents who are apraxia as one who simply "won't eat", "won't dress", or "wets himself". **Agnosia** is the inability to recognize familiar faces or objects. Many times these residents become agitated and combative, because they do not understand what is being asked of them or what they are being told to do. In response, they may dig in their heels and resist. From these descriptions, one can see that a person can be demented but not have psychotic symptoms such as schizophrenia or psychosis. Dementia most often develops in people who are in their 70's or older.

An important form of senile dementia is called **Alzheimer's disease,** which is a chronic, progressive and deteriorative brain disorder accompanied by profound effects on memory, cognition, and ability for self-care. With this disease, significant forgetfulness is common. Deterioration of higher cognitive function with confusion, disorientation, apathy, and stupor of various degrees can occur. There is also a possibility for the loss of ability to do his/her own ADL, eat, read, write, calculate, and eventually even to comprehend or speak intelligently. Alzheimer's disease can also result in personality changes and disorders of motor function, including abnormal gait and incontinence. They can be a danger to themselves due to their restlessness. It is the most common form of brain dysfunction among the aged, affecting more than two million elderly Americans.[36] Although some of them still remain at homes, many of them are residing in nursing homes. Today there are many facilities specifically designed to accommodate those with Alzheimer's disease.

Delusional: describes an individual who harbors suspicion and the idea of persecution without real reason. It is the second most common psychiatric disorder among the elderly, particularly those with sensory deficits and those who are loners. Sometimes with appropriate medications, hearing aids and glasses, the sense of isolation can be reduced. Episodes of delusion can also decrease.

Hallucination: a sensory perception, usually auditory in nature and occurs without reason. This person will hear sounds or voices. They often become afraid when they misperceive environmental stimuli. For example when they hear a loud sound, they may think that there is a break-in or a bomb going off, so they react in exaggerated ways.

Depression: a state of mind characterized by low mood, hopelessness, decreased sleep, loss of appetite, energy, and loss of interests. It may occur with or without dementia. Depression can also cause combativeness in a resident. This is the most common emotional disorder of the aged, occurring in 20-30% of the elderly.

II. Diagnoses

The use of chemical drugs for therapy is usually reserved for individuals who have schizophrenia or psychosis. However, there are many symptoms that are not truly related to mental illness, but are simply part of the dysfunction associated with aging. Excluded in the present consideration are truly mental disturbances such as psychosis, because these individuals are usually sent to state institutions. Instead this discussion will focus on those

---

[36]The Lippincott Manual of Nursing Practice, 4th edition. Reprinted with permission from J. B. Lippincott Co., Philadelphia, 1986, pp 896-897.

problems common to many residents in our nursing homes that are not mental illnesses, for which chemical restraints are nonetheless often used.

The first reason for a psychological problem is **mental impairment.** When a person is confused, disoriented, has poor eye sight, and is hard of hearing, his/her capacity to be able to communicate his/her thoughts and to understand the thoughts of others is impaired. Imagine that your loved one is in a deep sleep early in the morning. Somebody walks in and asks him/her to do something like take a shower. He/she is not given the chance to understand what the word "shower" is before his/her nightgown is being taken off without any explanation. He/she does not quite understand what is happening to him/her because of his/her cognitive impairment. If the staff tries to hurry him/her along, he/she might respond by becoming verbally abusive and striking out at the CNA. Yet this behavior is the result of the staff's impatience and lack of knowledge about the resident. Instead of using chemical restraints, it is important for the staff to realize that a cognitively impaired individual may exhibit these exaggerated reactions if he/she is not cared for properly. A simple, clear explanation must be given before anything is done to him/her. Give him/her time to respond to the request. The staff must be flexible and must know the limits of these residents. During task performance time, the staff should let the resident do the easy tasks and assist with the more complicated ones.

The second reason for a psychological problem that could lead to a catastrophic reaction is **anxiety.** Anxiety disorders are associated with the realization of loss of control over one's immediate environment. This includes the feeling of isolation, of being neglected, and of being rejected or unloved. The loss of independence, the fear of being a financial burden, of being in failing health, of having decreased intellectual functioning, and of having loss of friends, loved ones, home or pets also contribute to anxiety. These feelings are usually accompanied by a sense of helplessness and hopelessness. There could also be a fear of death and dying. Once again, it is up to the nurses to realize that anxiety is common in residents who do not have any organic mental illness. It is up to all the staff in the facility to do everything possible to reduce the causes for the anxiety.

The third reason for a psychological problem is **physical illnesses** - These include unrecognized or undiagnosed physical illnesses such as diabetes mellitus, congestive heart failure, infection, impending stroke, fecal impaction, and bladder infection. If any of these conditions are not yet diagnosed, the resident may become combative, confused and disoriented due to fever and dehydration. It is imperative that the CNA report any condition changes to the licensed nurses. In turn the nurse must serve as the resident's advocate in doing a thorough nursing assessment and in observing the specific behavior that was reported to her. He/she must encourage the physician to visit this resident, obtain an order for laboratory tests, and start appropriate treatments.

Since many treatable illnesses manifest as an acute confusional state, if there is early intervention, the condition will improve and subside. **Example:** An alert, oriented lady who is usually very quiet, cooperative, and independent complained of a painful, burning sensation when she urinates. She became incontinent, and the urine has a strong odor. She spiked a high fever, then became combative and belligerent. The CNA notified the Charge Nurse, and she in turn called the physician. He ordered emergency lab work, and the lab result showed that she had a urinary tract infection (bladder infection). He put her on an antibiotic immediately. Within days she recovered without any residual problems, and her temporary state of belligerence and incontinence subsided.

Finally the biggest contributor to psychological problems is **drug toxicity** - The average nursing home resident has what amounts to a "multi-drug pharmacy" or "polypharmacy". An example of polypharmacy is the excessive use of a stool softener and stimulant laxative in a resident who is experiencing constipation caused by pain medication such as codeine.[37] With this type of multiple medication regimen, the high incidence of drug-to-drug or drug-to-food interaction can be very real, resulting in severe, irreversible side effects. Some drugs can cause psychiatric symptoms which lead to behavior problems. Even an over-the-counter drug, Benadryl, when combined with other drugs, can cause anxiety, hallucinations or delirium.

Here is a non-obvious reason for over-medication. Unexpected family interaction can cause an undesirable reaction from a demented person. When his/her family members come to visit, the resident may not actually recognize them, or he/she may be carrying on an unrelated conversation, or he/she may be just making "gaa, gaa, gaa" noises. To avoid embarrassment, the family requests these drugs be given in order to control those sounds.[38]

III. Common Psychotropic Drugs

Some common psychotropic drugs often used as chemical restraints will be discussed below. If your loved one must use these drugs, you can monitor his/her response to the drug and be involved in his/her care. Regulations state that nurses of the facility will need to collaborate with the pharmacy consultant to monitor the effects of these drugs on each and every resident who has these prescriptions. The various categories of these drugs are psychotropic drugs, antidepressant drugs, antianxiety drugs, and hypnotic drugs (sleeping pills).

A. Psychotropic Drugs (chemical restraints). The prescription of these drugs is primarily meant to alter a

---

[37]Reprinted with permission from Simonson, William, *Mediations and the Elderly: A Guide for Promoting Proper Use.* Aspen Publication, 1984, p.32.
[38]Sherman, David S., Workshop on Reducing the Use of Chemical Restraints in Nursing Homes.Special Committee on Aging, U.S. Senate, Serial No. 102-6, 1991, p5.

person's mental function or control behavior. They are primarily used in the treatment of psychoses (mental disorders), such as **schizophrenia, paranoid psychoses, manic-depressive illness, delusional disorder, and organic brain syndrome (including delirium and dementia).** These drugs include: Haldol, Mellaril, Thorazine, Trilafon, Prolixin, Decanoate, Navane, Buspar, and Stelazine. It is a well-established fact that excessive use of these drugs can lead to significant irreversible side effects.[39]

Rebecca Elon, M.D., Medical Director of the Washington Home in Washington, D.C., stated that the three major drugs in this psychotropic group are **Haldol, Mellaril, and Thorazine.**[40] These drugs have been commonly called chemical restraints. When they are used appropriately these drugs actually facilitate, enable, or enhance an individual's functioning. However, only residents with psychiatric diagnoses can be put on these drugs.

Psychotropic drugs should not be used if one or more of the following behaviors is the only indication, or the behavior occurs intermittently. These include simple pacing, wandering, restlessness, crying out, yelling or screaming, impaired memory, anxiety, nervousness, depression, insomnia (unable to sleep), unsociability, indifference to surroundings, fidgeting, uncooperativeness, poor self-care, and nervousness. Any behavior which does not represent a danger to self or other residents does not require the use of these medications. If any of the above behaviors become continuous, and it starts to interfere with a resident's daily care, then the physician may prescribe a short-acting psychotropic drug for a limited time, with the lowest possible dose and with careful monitoring of side effects.

---

[39]Cadieux, Roger J., M.D., Geriatric psychopharmacology: The use of psychotropic drugs. In *Psychotropic Drugs and the Elderly Patient*, San Francisco Institute on Aging. 1992, pp3-14.

[40]Elon, Dr. Rebecca, Special Committee on Aging, U.S. Senate, Serial No. 102-6, p16, 1991

B. Antidepressant drugs: Drugs used for the treatment of depression. These include Atarax, Ativan, Elavil, Sinequan, Valium, Tofranil, Prozac, Pamelor, Norpramin, and Desyrele.

Example: A married couple was admitted to a nursing home at the same time. The husband had a history of unstable heart trouble and was in poor health. One day his condition changed for the worse, and he was transferred to an acute hospital in critical condition. The next day the wife found out that her husband had died in the acute hospital. She became very depressed. She cried constantly, lost interest in eating, neglected her own personal care, and refused to use the bathroom; she became incontinent. When the CNA asked her to do some of her own activities of daily living (dressing, bathing, grooming, eating, or walking), she refused to do them. The CNA continued to insist, and a confrontation occurred. She became verbally abusive, uncooperative and combative toward staff. In this case, the nursing staff was aware of the problem that caused her behavior change from a cordial and cooperative person to an irrational one. Consequently, the Charge Nurse discussed the situation with the Social Service Director, who then helped the resident go through the bereavement process. The resident requested short-term use of a mood elevator drug. Her physician was called, and he agreed to prescribe an antidepressant drug to relieve the symptoms.

C. Antianxiety drugs: Drugs used for the treatment of nervousness and mood changes. These are Ativan, Librium, Serax, Xanax, Valium, Klonopin, Restoril, and Halcion.

Example: An alert and oriented post-stroke gentleman is constantly worried about his finances, fearing he is being a burden to his family and frustrated by not being able to hear clearly. When people talk to him, he cannot understand the words. He kept all these problems to himself, and that caused him not to be able to sleep at night, so he started to get up later and later each day. This caused emotional and social problems with the family, because his schedule was not the same as the rest of them. After consulting with his physician, a mood elevator drug was prescribed for him, and he is slowly improving his attitude toward life. He started to do more and more for himself.

D. Hypnotic agents: Drugs used for the treatment of sleeplessness. They are Dalmane, Meprobamate, Phenobarbital, Halcion, and Seconal. Some of the antianxiety and antihistamine drugs can be used for sleeplessness as well.

Example: An alert and oriented lady lives alone after her husband became incapacitated. She cannot sleep well at night, so she decided to take her husband's prescribed hypnotic medication (halcion) as an aid for her own sleeplessness. As time went by, side effects appeared. Her memory started to slowly deteriorate, and her head and hands developed fine tremors. Her family noted this change and asked what medicines she is on. When it was discovered that she had been taking her husband's medication without prescription, the staff carefully examined the side effects of this medication. One of the most noticeable side effects of this medication is poor memory. She immediately stopped taking this medication and changed her lifestyle to decrease her anxiety, allowing her to sleep better.

IV. Side effects:

The principal side effects from these drugs are dry mouth, hypotension (low blood pressure when standing up from a chair or getting out of the bed), urinary retention, constipation which can lead to impaction of stool, drowsiness, nervousness, restlessness or the need to keep moving, unsteadiness on feet, loss of balance, gait, and positioning ability, involuntary movement, trembling of the hands and fingers, confusion, incontinence of bladder, dependency on the drug (habit forming), weight gain, and blurred vision. The worst side effect is **tardive dyskinesia.** The earliest sign is an individual sticking the tip of his/her tongue out involuntarily. If not detected early these symptoms may produce irreversible damages including involuntary jerking, thrusting movements of the hands, head, feet, face, tongue, lips, and/or chewing puckering movements of the mouth. You can obtain more detailed information about side effects of the specific drug prescribed for your loved one from your pharmacist, physician and the nurses in the facility.

V. What can you do?

Given the above listed side effects, if you have a loved one in a nursing home who is about to receive any of these types of medication, make sure you understand the "why" of these drugs. The questions to ask are: Is there a physician's order for the drug? Is there a diagnosis that warrants the use of such a drug? Is the restraint used for behavior control or to prevent falls? Does the order identify the specific behavior for the use of the drug? Does the order identify what type and when the drug is to be used? Since all of us respond differently to medication, does the nursing home staff have some special mechanism to monitor whether the medication actually helped or harmed my loved one? Are Physical or Occupational Therapists involved initially and periodically in the evaluation and re-evaluation for alternative measures? Have all non-chemical means been exhausted before the chemical restraint was prescribed?

Before any mood controlling drugs can be used, the **target behaviors** must be observed by the nursing staff on all shifts and be documented in the Nurses' Notes for seventy-two hours. Target behaviors include: kicking, biting, scratching, hitting, pulling tubes out, yelling, and screaming continuously. When a resident exhibits these behaviors, the interdisciplinary team must do a complete assessment on the resident to identify the cause. Is it a result of drug toxicity, physical illness, staff impatience, roommate incompatibility, or interaction with the family members? During this evaluation period, alternative methods of control should be experimented with. Steps to eliminate or reduce the causes, as well as how to implement the new approaches should be discussed in the Care Plan conference by the interdisciplinary team. If all else fails, a psychiatric consultant's assessment should be initiated. The slogan for the use of drug therapy should be **"go low and go slow"**, then gradually increase the dosage and frequency if needed. If the behavior is still not controlled, you must ask your loved one's physician to have a consultation with the pharmacist and a psychiatrist to devise another plan of treatment. Do not let the staff tell you to just "let it go" without further intervention.

VI. Commentary: A pattern of misuse

The vast majority of residents of nursing homes who are receiving chemical drugs do not suffer from psychosis, but in fact are elderly individuals with dementia. A recent study reported in Journal of American Geriatrics Society concluded that for people with dementia, the use of these medications is only moderately effective (about 20% of the time) in improving the targeted behaviors.[41] Despite such statistics and stringent regulations, a study by David S. Sherman found that psychotropic drug use pattern in our nation's nursing homes demonstrates a continued lack of awareness among our physicians, nurses, and pharmacists.[42] In fact, the use of these drugs is not only not very helpful in many of the elderly residents but downright dangerous. He also stated that federal laws mandated that there be consulting pharmacists in nursing homes to monitor medications and to give information on drugs to residents, staff, and family members. But the sad fact is that in most nursing homes across the country, this still is not happening. The decision of whether to start, increase, decrease or

---

[41]Reprinted with permission from Schneider, Lon S., et al., JAGS 38: 553-563, 1990.

[42]Sherman, David S.,J. Phamacy Practices 1: 189-194, 1988.

discontinue a psychotropic medication is based on a trial or error method, because the physicians do not have a reliable data base or daily monitoring information upon which to form their decisions. When the physician orders psychotropic medications inappropriately we are doing something that causes more harm than good for the residents.

A study published in the New England Journal of Medicine about five years ago found that nursing home residents who take psychotropic drugs are two or three times more likely to experience a fractured hip.[43] According to the American Psychiatric Association in 1979, at least 40% of elderly people who are placed on these medications are likely to develop some form of side effects, including tardive dyskinesia.[44]

Why is the inappropriate use of these drugs still prevalent? To get a sense of the problem, we must first look at the fact that many of the residents are transferred into the nursing home with these psychotropic medications already on the physician's order sheet. These patients may have needed some of these drugs to alleviate acute conditions while they were in the acute hospital. If the transfer order sheet was not scrutinized carefully by the licensed nurses in the nursing home, then the psychotropic mediation is simply carried over without questions being asked. Secondly, we must look at the mental profile of nursing home residents. Among those confined to the nursing home the prevalence of psychiatric behavior disorder has been estimated to range from 68 to 94 percent. It is of interest to note that in a recent survey, of the 454 new admissions into various nursing homes of this sample, over 67 percent of these are considered to be "demented" in some way or form, and an additional 12

---

[43]cf. footnote 38, p4.
[44]*ibid.*

percent have other psychiatric disorders.[45] On the surface, then, we would think of these nursing homes as mental institutions, and therefore the treatment method of using antipsychotic drugs is correct. Dr. Rovner, Professor of Psychiatry and Behavior Science at Johns Hopkins University, proceeds to analyze this situation more carefully and finds that the use of antipsychotic drugs on upwards of 40 percent of the "demented" residents is excessive and in many cases, inappropriate.[46]

Dr. Rebecca Elon, M.D., testified that before OBRA 1987, the use of psychotropic drugs by physicians and licensed nurses was a medical and private issue. After OBRA 1987, it has become a public issue, and one that is debated openly.[47] She went on to cite that in a January, 1991 issue of the Journal of the American Medical Association, it was stated that about half of the residents in the nursing homes on these drugs did not have an appropriate diagnosis or a specific condition to justify their use.[48] Therefore, about half of the drug use would be considered inappropriate. Some of the reasons that residents in a nursing home are over-medicated with psychotropic drugs will be examined:

Most of the nursing home facilities have a monthly pharmacy consultant visit to review the usage of psycho-tropic drugs. It is then up to the Director of Nursing and the licensed nurses to communicate these results with each resident's physician, even though nurses often fear the wrath of the physicians. Nurses must be on the alert to observe for side effects of the medication, be it drooling, shaking, having trouble swallowing, or being unable to stay awake or sit still. What the physician needs are nurses who demonstrate

---

[45]Reprinted with permission from Rovner, Barry W., MD, et al., International Psychogeriatrics 2: 13-24, 1990.

[46]ibid.

[47]Elon, Rebecca, M.D., Special Committee on Aging of the U.S. Senate. Serial 102-6, pp17-21.

[48]Garrard, Judith, et al., JAMA 265:463-467, 1991.

knowledge and skills in assessment to serve as their on-site
"eyes", and then are able to communicate to the physicians
with clarity, precision and conviction. Licensed nurses must
be brave enough to ask the physician if the observed
symptoms could be due to the medication, and whether the
dose of the medication could be lowered. Too often, these
questions are not asked.

Another reason for over-medicating nursing home
residents is the fact that licensed nurses and certified nursing
assistants are over-worked, underpaid, and over-stressed.
With a heavy load of 10 to 25 residents per CNA, and
licensed nurses who have even more residents under their
care per shift, it is very difficult for the staff to provide the
highest level of quality of care for all of them. The result is if
a resident does not fit into the expected mode of behavior,
restraints become the course of care. Frustration and anger
often occur as does a high "burnout" and turnover rate. The
CNAs who work in nursing homes are as a group the most
unheralded people in our work force. It is a case of the
disenfranchised taking care of the disenfranchised.

Nursing assistants complain that they do not have
enough time to do a lot of things that they really want to do.
These include giving back rubs, cleaning dentures
thoroughly, giving better oral care and spending more time
with the alert, oriented residents. Most of their time is spent
on those who are in need of total care, those who are
confused and disoriented, the very old, the
uncommunicative and the unresponsive. The licensed nurses
also occasionally neglect to monitor the behavior problems,
so the data in the drug monitoring flow sheet are not
absolutely accurate or up-to-date. They spend much time
often concentrating on complying with various mandatory
paperwork instead of focusing on the residents' daily quality
of care. For most nurses, their job evaluations and increased
pay depend on their paperwork, not their humanitarian
assets. They are not allowed to prioritize in favor of resident

care they do not receive the appropriate training to do this challenging job.

Another contributing factor to over-medication is that most physicians have been trained in the acute care hospitals and carry what has been taught to them as the standard of practice into nursing homes. Their prescriptions often are connected with specific diseases, not the wellness of the whole being. Physicians have been entrusted with the legal authority, the responsibility, the liability, and hopefully the education and training for prescribing medications for individual geriatric residents. But in this environment, the total psychosocial aspects must be given heavier weight among other medical considerations. The staff and the pharmacy consultant must be willing to work with these physicians in promoting the total health of residents.

Currently, nursing homes are trying to take a leadership role in decreasing the inappropriate use of antipsychotic medications for elderly residents. Many facilities are attempting to taper off the use of these drugs. The staff need to realize that their residents deserve the best medical care. This is where you, as the family member, can also help the facility's staff achieve a chemical restraint-free environment by not requesting the physician give your loved one a mood-controlling medication. The staff should not be afraid to set high standards and to work with physicians through strong, positive interactions. They have to realize that they can break the pattern of negative interactions between staff and physicians in nursing homes and move forward with quality medical leadership to implement the guidelines of OBRA 1987.

To show that positive actions can and have been taken, several incidents of positive action initiated by the nursing staff in a nursing home that led to a reduction in chemical restraints are cited:

Example #1: An elderly resident only screams in the morning and at night when the CNA performs ADL for her and gets her in and out of bed. Otherwise she is quiet and attends various activities. Her antipsychotic medications were prescribed from the acute hospital, and no one bothered to discontinue the medications when she was admitted to the convalescent hospital. From her clinical records the interdisciplinary team and the pharmacy consultant could not find a justification for this medication. After conferring with the doctor, many of the psychotropic medications were reduced both in dosage and in frequency. Others were totally eliminated after several months of gradual reduction. Her episodes of screaming became less frequent. This was a case of excessive medication leading to the behavior problem.

Example #2: A Caucasian lady in her late sixties was transferred from a local acute hospital to a skilled nursing facility along with medication for treating numerous medical problems. At least five of them were for inappropriate behaviors. There was no specific psychiatric or behavior disorder diagnosis and no clinical documentation. The nursing staff was ordered to watch for involuntary movements of the body and extremities and to notify the physician. In time, the staff found that she had trouble controlling her upper body and was unsteady when walking. She was frequently found sitting or lying on the floor but never injured herself. She would scream and cry out without provocation and was combative. She was very strong physically. The pharmacy consultant recommended evaluation of all the drugs. The Director of Nursing suggested the pharmacy consultant's recommendations to the physician, but the physician refused to do anything about it. Instead, he said to bring this case to his attention at his visit next month. At that time, the Director of Nursing again brought up the situation with the doctor. This time the physician agreed with the staff and eliminated some medications and reduced other medication both in dosage and frequency. The resident's behavior improved considerably. She was able to communicate with the staff and walked with control; she also started putting make-up and lipstick on her face. She recognized her husband for the first time. She became less combative. Most of her involuntary movements slowly went away. She even told the staff and the physician that the medication had made her act in a certain way, and she was helpless to make it right. She told the physician she knew exactly which medication caused the problems and which helped her. The physician was surprised but was happy to have such an active participant.

Example #3: A Caucasian lady had a diagnosis of schizophrenia, but had not exhibited any abnormal behavior for 90 days. She was very cooperative, going to the dining room to eat her meals, and attending all the activities. The pharmacy consultant recommended putting her on a drug reduction (both quantity and frequency) regimen. The Director of Nursing then worked with the physician to follow the consultant's recommendation. After a week of the trial period her symptoms started to appear. She started to hallucinate frequently, become paranoid, and inflicting wounds on her face, nose and hands. When asked by the staff why she was doing this, she replied, "There are bugs on my body and I must remove them." The licensed nurse called the physician and the medication was put back. This specific medication (Haldol 1 mg three days a day) was correct for her diagnosis and condition. This in turn was documented by the physician in her clinical record.

An inappropriate drug usage incident

An article appearing in the Sacramento Bee reported that an elderly woman who checked into a nursing home for an eight-week recovery program after hip surgery was allegedly kept against her will for three years through powerful drugs that reduced her to a semi-vegetative state.[49] "It does not pay to be feisty in a nursing home," stated

---

[49]Coronado, Ramon, "Nursing home sued over use of mind-altering drugs". *Sacramento Bee*, Dec. 10, 1993, p.B4

Russell S. Balisok, the lawyer who filed the suit on behalf of the patient. The patient apparently received mind-altering drugs such as Thorazine, Mellaril, and Prolixin for no medical reasons. She was drugged into a stupor for behavior control. The suit alleges that due to these drugs she was left in a daze, so incapacitated that she could not feed herself, and a nasogastric tube had to be inserted into her stomach. On one occasion, a staff nurse gave her too much fluid, and her stomach could not hold that. It backed up into her lungs, causing an immediate heart attack that led to her comatose state.

This above cited example is one of the most serious and sad cases. Unfortunately, it is not a case in isolation. When an elderly resident is confused and disoriented, yelling and screaming, the staff will say he/she is either crazy or demented. They will insist that he/she be put on some drugs to control those behaviors. What is frightening is that once a resident is branded as being demented, he/she will be treated like a patient/resident who has a psychiatric disorder. To prevent inappropriate treatment, the physician must conduct a comprehensive physical examination, call for medical and psychological assessments, and order various tests to find out what are the underlying causes in order to differentiate demented behavior from true psychotic behavior. Only then can a prescription be issued that is appropriate for treating the specific behavior problem based on that diagnosis.

If you suspect violations on the part of the staff in the use of chemical restraints on your loved one, make sure your suspicions are made known. You need to talk first with the Nursing Supervisor, the Director of Nursing, and the Administrator. You can request information from the resident's clinical record. The facility must comply with your request within a reasonable time. If this is unsatisfactory, consult with your loved one's physician, and the pharmacy consultant. The State Ombudsman is the next level of access in case of need. Finally the state certification and licensing office can be reached. You can remain anonymous when voicing your concerns. The state must respond to your complaint within three days by visiting the facility. No facility cherishes these visits by the state.

Equal to importance of being chemical restraint-free is being physical restraint-free. In the next chapter, the focus will again be on why many residents are being restrained (physically). This two chapters are closely interrelated. An individual can become very aggressive and combative when his/her freedom and autonomy has been violated. in odor to control this inappropriate behavior, the CNA will tell the licensed nurse about the incidence. The next thing you know is that your loved one has being put on a new drug to control the problem. It can go the other way, which is to apply a restraint. I strong believe that a thorough assessment must be done before any action is taken. You can help by asking questions to assure that your loved one has been given every chance to be free from those restraints.

CHAPTER 10

Physical Restraints

OBRA Guideline on the Use of Physical Restraint 155
Responsibilities for Fall Prevention 156
Types of Physical Restraints 162
Evaluation of Resident for Physical Restraint 164
Restraint Elimination 165
    Steps to Take for Fall Prevention 165
    Options for the Reduction of Restraints 167

A There is no consensus about what constitutes a restraint. For the present purpose, **physical restraint** will be defined in the OBRA 87 manner. Physical restraint is any manual method or mechanical device, material, or equipment attached to or adjacent to a resident's body that restricts the freedom, movement or normal access to his/her body. The restraint is designed so that the individual cannot remove it easily. OBRA regulations are very clear about the unnecessary use of physical restraints. Specifically, regulation (in boldface) states that **all residents have the right to be free from any physical restraints imposed for the purposes of discipline, convenience or when they are not required to treat medical symptoms. The facility must implement procedures that protect a resident from abuse, neglect and mistreatment when physical restraints are used.**

This chapter will explore what is necessary in terms of attitudes, skills, and resources to provide nursing home care without physical restraints. In particular, some of the medical and legal barriers to treating residents with the care and dignity that they deserve will be explored.

There are over 16,000 nursing homes in this country. It takes money and much more effort than simply setting up regulations to achieve a restraint-free environment. Arnold Silverman suggests three areas of action in order to attain a restraint-free environment.[50] These are responsibility, inputs and options. Facilities often cite the problems of residents with unsteady gait falling and injuring themselves, and those wandering out of the facility or getting out of the bed by themselves without assistance as the primary reasons for the use of restraints. However, according to the late Senator John Heinz, when restraints are used, the resident deteriorates much more rapidly and sacrifices his/her physical and mental health, vitality, and most of all his/her human dignity.[51] He believes that the conventional wisdom (of fall prevention) is wrong, and that there are humane, caring alternatives to strapping residents into wheelchairs or beds.

Responsibilities for fall prevention:
Nursing home staff personnel, the residents as well as their responsible parties must be equally concerned. We have all heard horror stories of the unnecessary use of restraints on residents leading to death. The questions you should ask the staff are:
1. What constitutes a restraint?
2. Is there a physician's order for the restraint?
3. What type of restraint is being ordered?
4. What part of the body will it restrain? For how long?
5. Why do you want to restrain my loved one?
6. Does my loved one want to be restrained?
7. Is this particular restraint the most appropriate method for my loved one.

---

[50]Silverman, Arnold, President, Skil-Care Corp., In testimony of the Special Committee on Aging, U.S. Senate, 1989, Serial No. 101-H, p19
[51]Heinz, Hon. John, Senator, Pennsylvania. In opening statement of the Special Committee on Aging, U.S. Senate, 1989, Serial No. 101-H, p1

8. Were all alternative means tried before this decision is made?
9. Who signed the consent order?

Facilities do have a responsibility to keep their residents safe from falls. It has been the historical argument that the use of physical restraints is the surest way of preventing falls and injuries to residents. Injuries from falls are the immediate reason for many elderly person's admissions to nursing homes. However, as Marshall Kapp argues, the fear of legal liability is often used as a pretext for using restraints when in fact their use is based on "professional bias, staff convenience, behavior control and... financial incentives."[52]

Since falls are attributable to environmental hazards, it is necessary to recognize that an environment that appears to be safe for a fully functioning adult presents hazards to the ambulatory but frailer, older resident who requires custodial care. The most inhabited environment for an elderly resident is in his/her own room or the bathroom, and in fact most of the accidents occur in these two places. There are non-restraining methods that will be listed to make that environment safer, thus preventing these accidents.

Nearly a quarter of the falls are attributable to physical conditions such as arthritis, loss of balance, dizziness and collapsed knees (buckled knee). The older resident very possibly also has poor vision, one or more chronic ailments such as heart disease, high blood pressure, orthostatic hypo-tension (sudden low blood pressure when standing up from a chair or bed too fast), diabetes, Parkinson's disease or the residual effects of a stroke. Drugs used to treat these diseases can increase the risk of falling directly or indirectly through their drug toxicity. There are also mounting data showing that the chance of an injurious

---

[52]Kapp, Marshall, in testimony of the Special Committee on Aging, U.S. Senate, 1989, Serial No. 101-H, p29.

fall actually can increase with the prolonged use of mechanical restraints.[53]

In addition, medications given to many elderly people to counter depression, dementia or insomnia can result in confusion, disorientation, and coordination difficulties that add to the risk of falling. Researchers have found that those who fall have significantly weaker muscles than those who do not fall. They also found that many residents for whom walkers have been prescribed do not use them because they consider them more of an impediment than an aid to mobility. Many of the mobility assisting devices do require some adjustment, and there should be a physical therapist working with the resident on his/her new equipment until he/she masters the proper technique. Support devices and restraints, when properly used in times of need, can be considered marvelous tools. However, a preventive measure that robs the dignity of the resident should never be tolerated.

Often, after a fall the elderly person may impose a voluntary restriction of activity leading to a loss of mobility, self-confidence and independence. Such self-imposed restricted activity also leads to a decline in physical strength, which further increases the risk of falling. Even in the nursing home where the environment has been arranged for the safety of people with limited physical ability and agility, the risk of falling persists.

Fall prevention aside, a vast majority of residents in a nursing home are unable to speak and are mentally or physically impaired. Often they are unable to sign papers for themselves and do not have the ability to express their wishes to others. Sometimes a resident admitted into this strange environment may exhibit some inappropriate behaviors. Such behaviors may be the result of staff impatience, or it could be due to his/her having heard other residents screaming or making loud outbursts. Physical

---

[53]*ibid*, p.30.

restraints are often introduced at these times of extreme physical and emotional distress, ostensibly to prevent his/her agitation from reaching a "catastrophic reaction". However, the following scenario can easily take place: Being mentally impaired, the resident does not understand why he/she is being tied to his/her bed or chair, and he/she becomes increasingly more anxious and perturbed. He/she manipulates these ties and calls out for help to no avail. This often leads to terror, frustration and anger, which lead to verbal abusiveness and combativeness. When the staff sees the resident behaving in this fashion, they become more convinced that the restraint is necessary for the resident's own safety. From the resident's perspective, when the protest does not result in freedom, the fighting often subsides, followed by the attitudes of resignation and withdrawal. The resident will often detach himself intellectually and emotionally and move to a level of existence that we have little or no hope of reversing. This is typical of what we see in our nursing homes today. Restraints may have saved some residents from potential physical injury, but they definitely have also robbed them of their self-dignity and independence.

Unfortunately, like this example, there are too many frail, old people in the nursing homes throughout the United States who are routinely tied to their beds and/or their chairs, left to struggle, complain and plead to be free. They may even end up spending their entire day concentrating on nothing but getting loose from the physical restraint. By their being reduced to doing this, they are becoming emotionally and physically more frail and drained.

It is important to realize that a misinterpretation of the condition of a resident can definitely result in the resident being placed in the category of having behavior problems, consequently receiving unnecessary restraints to control a perceived aggressive behavior, which was sometimes caused by the staff in the first place. It is therefore the responsibility of the staff to guard against these misinterpretations.

What we have seen is that restraints can cause gross emotional and psychosocial deterioration as well as physical problems[54]:

1. Increased tendency to exhibit complete dependence on the staff.
2. Increased symptoms of withdrawal or depression.
3. Increased tendency for the individual to reduce social contact.
4. Increased chance of bowel and bladder incontinence.
5. Decreased range of motion.
6. Increased contractures.
7. Decreased ability to ambulate.
8. Slowed intestinal activity leading to chronic constipation.
9. Loss of minerals from their bones.
10. Muscles which become weak and nonfunctioning.
11. Decreased appetite.
12. Increased frequency of pressure ulcers and sores.

The administrators and nurses currently are caught in a vise between the advocates for less restraint application on the one hand, and the insurance companies, lawyers and families who would not hesitate to sue in case of a fall, on the other hand. Studies have shown that lawsuits are not successfully prosecuted against facilities solely for failure to restrain a resident. The family must prove that an improper assessment of the resident was made, or there was a failure to monitor the restraint appropriately, or there was a failure to respond to the fall in a timely and professionally acceptable manner[55]. With full documentation of the risks and benefits of restraints that includes the resident and

---

[54]Burger, Sarah, Detrimental effects of physical and chemical restraints on residents. National Center for State Long Term Care Ombudsman Resources, pp.56-61, 1989.
[55]cf. footnote 52, p.29.

family members in the decision making process, litigation will probably decrease.

The nursing home industry often claims that the care given is the best they can do under the financial circumstances. It is true that we can continue to regulate the nursing home industry forever and ever, but until we recognize the fact that caring for our frail elderly takes more resources, time and attention than we have been able to provide, we will have little hope of meeting the intent of these regulations. The argument here is that even though the industry realizes that restraints make residents more frail and in the long run, will demand more hours of care, there is little that can be done unless programs such as Medicaid can support the nursing homes at a higher per diem rate than the current situation.

Having seen how over-worked most of the CNAs are in a nursing home, I agree that caring for the restrained resident requires more time than presently allocated. At present, the minimum number of hours per patient per day that a nursing home is required to allot is 3.0 hours, whereas a more personalized care approach would require an average of 3.5 to 4.0 hours. Unfortunately, knowing how the facilities operate, I do not think any facility is willing to go up to 3.5 or 4.0 hours per patient per day given today's Medicaid reimbursement rate.

We must somehow strike a balance between absolute safety and respect for the individual's dignity and human rights. The conventional way of doing things is wrong. We must change our attitudes, skills, and resources to provide nursing home care with dignity, and we must break down the barriers, medical, legal, and practical, to treating residents with the care and the kindness they deserve. We should stop blaming and suing somebody for the falls some of the residents will sustain. The elimination of physical restraints is the single most important factor that can improve the quality of life and quality of care in nursing facilities across the nation. A physical restraint is in direct conflict to autonomy, and its use undermines the ability of the staff to perceive and interact with the older person as an individual.

Decision Inputs on Using Restraints:

In this general area, different sources of inputs to decision-making will be provided. Lynne Mitchell-Pedersen identified four categories of behaviors that are most likely to result in the use of restraints.[56] These are people who:

1. exhibit unsafe mobility and are at risk for falls when walking.

2. exhibit disruptive or aggressive behavior toward others.

3. interfere with life support systems, primarily his/her own.

4. wander in or out of restricted areas.

The only other circumstance when a resident might be in need of a physical restraint is when he/she needs postural support and special positioning.

Types of physical restraints:

A list of the more commonly used physical restraints follows:

1. The lap belt - This is like a car seat belt with a buckle release.

2. The posey vest or crossover vest (houdini) - This resembles a vest with a long cord for tying behind the chair or bed to prevent falls, or to prevent them from getting out of bed or chair. When using this type of restraint the CNAs are taught to make sure the knot is tied in a bow style and not as a "dead knot" for emergency release purposes. To protect your loved

[56]Mitchell-Petersen, Lynne, Clinical Nurse Specialist in Geriatric Nursing, St. Boniface General Hospital, Winnipeg, Manitoba, Canada. In testimony of the Special Committee on Aging, U.S. Senate, 1989, Serial No. 101-H, 50.

one, it is also important that the opening of this vest is in the front while the high neckline is towards the back. This will prevent possible choking or strangulation.

3. The pelvic crotch restraint - This device is used to keep people from sliding out of their wheelchair. If they slide forward the device will automatically become tighter. If used improperly, the tightness can cause injury.

4. Wrist restraints - Usually made out of Velcro material to restrain movement of hands and arms. This is used to prevent a resident from pulling out his own NG, GT, IV or Foley catheter tubes.

5. Wheelchairs with a roll bar and an attached harness - Such a device will keep the user from slipping down in his/her chair.

6. Geri-chair with a tray across the front.

7. Bedside rails.

8. Bedside slings.

9. Sheet tucked in so tightly that a bed-bound resident cannot move.

10. Placing a wheelchair-bound resident so close to a wall that the wall prevents the resident from rising.

As one who is concerned about the welfare of your loved one in a facility, if you do not want any restraints placed on him/her then sign "No" on the "Restraint Consent form". This should be your initial input into the use or non-use of physical restraints. Do not let the facility's personnel talk you into a "yes" on this form. Since it usually takes an individual two to three weeks to get used to a new idea or a totally new and strange environment, wait at least 14 to 21 days after the admission to discuss any type of restraints with the staff. This will give enough time for an interdisciplinary team to do a complete assessment (see the section on MDS).

Evaluation of resident for physical restraint

Before the use of a physical restraint, an occupational or physical therapist must first be consulted regarding various types of less restrictive interventions to be tried. The staff must observe the resident 24 hours a day for 3 days. This means day shift, PM shift, and night shift personnel all have responsibilities to monitor the resident's specific behavior. The behavior must be documented in the nurse's notes. In all cases, since restraints can cause potential and real side effects, there must be a specific reason and a time frame for their use. Secondly, every effort must be made to limit the use of physical restraints to less than 12 hours a day, unless the resident's condition warrants longer duration. Thirdly, all restrained residents must be checked every thirty minutes and released at least every two hours for ten minutes during normal waking hours, and two to four hours at night to allow the resident to move and do range-of-motion exercise either actively or passively. If the restraint is necessary the staff must tell the resident and the family members the potential side effects and negative aspects of this method. Every restrained resident must also be reviewed at least quarterly for the Restraint Elimination Program by the interdisciplinary team.

Not all residents are candidates for the restraint-free system, but every situation is unique and must be treated on an individual basis. In order to reduce or totally eliminate restraints we need to have inputs from the residents, family members, Administrators, Board of Directors, Department heads, staff, and physicians in the form of a pre-intervention survey questionnaire to find out how each person feels about restraints, the concerns they have, and why they feel it is important to use or not to use them. With the inputs gathered the Director of Staff Development can then educate all of them why restraints are sometimes unnecessary and what the alternatives are.

The staff will receive inputs through education. Generally, this will be by using in-service education classes, resident's council, family council, slide presentations, support groups, problem-solving sessions and one-on-one consultations. The staff need the facility Administrator's and its Director of Nursing's full support in order to be successful in attempting to reduce or to eliminate physical restraints.

In one facility where I worked as Nursing Supervisor and as Director of Nursing, I had the full support of the Administrator and the staff. She gave me permission to buy several less restrictive devices to use on four residents. We eliminated the vest restraints and applied foam wedges onto the wheelchair for these residents. These residents enjoyed the softness of the cushions, and there were no falls. In fact one of the residents even stopped yelling and started to attend activities. In this case, the elimination of restraints actually resulted in freeing up nursing staff time that was used solely to manage the use of those restraints.

Steps to take for fall prevention, which in turn will eliminate restraints.

These points are equally important for the staff as well as for you who frequent the facilities and notice many potential hazards.

1. Keep hallways free of obstacles.
2. Wipe up all spills on the floors immediately, and thoroughly, then put a large, yellow "wet" sign over the spot or rope off the area until it dries.
3. Equip bathrooms with grab-bars around the toilet, the tub and the shower. Use glued-on non-slip strips or animal figures in showers or tubs. Use shower bench and hand held shower head.
4. Keep stairways well lit and cover steps with non-skid treads mark top and bottom steps with glow-in-the-dark tape.
5. Place night lights on the route between the bed and the bathroom. Leave a light on in the bathroom at night.

6. Do not wax the floor. Waxing makes the floor very glossy and slippery.
7. Ensure that all shoes and slippers have non-slip rubber soles.
8. Make sure residents' glasses and hearing aids are in workable condition and that they are wearing these.
9. Develop a daily exercise and ambulation and creative restorative program for the residents.
10. Take the resident to the bathroom before and after meals, and at least every two hours during other times.
11. Put the call-bell within easy reach of the resident.
12. Have all staff personnel continuously reassess residents to determine the need for the use of a restraint or to eliminate it.
13. Have the same nursing assistant care for the same group of residents consistently month after month if feasible.
14. For wanderers, use yellow strips across the doorway, and put audio-visual notification in the form of "wander guard" on the wrist or legs. Have "stop" signs posted at the entry door and the dining room door with an activating alarm. Have french door installed.
15. Set up rocking chairs with foot stools along the hallways as resting places for wandering residents.
16. Use a triangle elevation wedge cushions in front to prevent sliding or falling forward. Use pillow pads between the knees, and foam cushions or foam wedges for support of the back. This alleviates local aches and pains. Bending a bed-ridden resident's knees when he/she is on his/her side will make it easier for him/her to maintain that position.
17. Make wheelchair or seating chairs comfortable such that the resident's feet are able to touch the footrest or floor.
18. Use anti-tipping plastic devices for wheelchairs either in the front or at the back depending on which way the resident likes to tip.

19. Have food tray close to the resident to prevent reaching out too far. Assist or feed those who cannot feed themselves.
20. Provide low beds or put mattresses on the floor.
21. Do not move resident's furniture or belongings without first notify him/her.

Options designed for the reduction of restraints:

Knowing all of the options available for the reduction or elimination of physical restraints is paramount in importance. If many or all of these options are put into use, it is reasonable to believe facilities can become restraint-free environments.

1. Release the restraint under the supervision of the staff during meal time and activity program time for an hour, two to three times a day. In fact, all family members who are at the dining room can also help with the supervision. In other words, even when considered justified and necessary, physical restraints can be released when there is proper attention and supervision.
2. For those residents who are bedridden, assist them in changing their positions every two hours. This practice is good for the circulation and decreases the chances of developing pressure sores. Keeping their perianal area clean and dry after each incontinence episode decreases the chance of skin inflammation and irritation. Getting them out of bed and bringing them out of their room for a change of scene will give them comfort and a sense of belonging.
3. When the residents become noisy and restless or complains of being hungry or thirsty, give him/her water or warm milk and crackers. A warm shower or a walk around the hallways can also soothe a person, as does soothing and diversionary radio programs. Reduce or eliminate caffeine drinks after seven o'clock in the evening.

4. Involve family members in their care before the resident goes to sleep if feasible.
5. Let the residents know there are staff on duty twenty-four hours a day, seven days a week to reduce anxiety at night.
6. Educate the staff to the elderly resident's mental and physical limitations. Whenever the nursing staff personnel does anything for a resident, especially at night, he or she should be sure that the resident is awake and understands the simple instructions before proceeding with a procedure. Always give clear, calm, self-assured verbal instructions. Allow ample time for the resident to respond. Call him/her by his/her name and tell him/her who you are. Use a night light or a flashlight to give care at night. Do not turn the overhead light on unless absolutely necessary.
7. For alert and oriented residents, the PVC walker with a seat attached to the back and a soft leg divider to separate the legs can be used during independent walking. The front bar has a knob for the resident to open and close by himself whenever the need arises.
8. When a resident complains, be attentive and check the resident's surroundings to see if there is a way to remove or correct those conditions that might be producing the upsetting situation.
9. Hugging or giving a little peck on the cheek to a somewhat flustered resident will indicate that everything is all right. Ask him/her exactly what happened and give him/her ample time to respond to those questions.
10. Establish and tailor staff and family visiting programs to periods of agitation to help calm the resident.
11. Arrange for volunteers to bring pet animals to the facility for visits as these visits have been shown to have significant therapeutic value.

Summary:
Everyone involved in the care of the residents has a responsibility for the resident's safety, comfort, health and dignity. This responsibility is shared among staff, physicians, family members, advocates of restraint-free facilities, lawmakers, and manufacturers. There are many fine facilities across our country that are working very hard to meet and exceed the accepted and mandated standards of practices. They are trying to create a restraint-free environment for the very special people who live in the nursing homes in the country. They are trying to untie the elderly and to give them quality care without restraints.

On the other extreme, deficient facilities certainly do exist. If you have a complaint or see a violation, you can call and report the information to the nursing staff, any department heads, the administrator, the state licensing and certification division or the state Ombudsman representing that facility's residents. Do not ignore this important task. You are the guardians of these most vulnerable residents in the facilities.

In order to more fully appreciate the breadth of the problems that beset nursing homes, it is time to consider the following question. Since this book has already spelled out the many ways of assuring high quality of life and care and of doing away with most of the chemical and physical restraints, why is it that most nursing homes are still operating at a mediocre level at best? An insider's perspective is given in the last chapter.

CHAPTER 11

Problem Areas and Potential Solutions

Are There No Improvements?..170
Nursing Department Problems..172
      Certified Nursing Assistants 173
      Licensed Vocational Nurses 179
      Supervisors..182
      Director of Nursing..183
Physicians 188
General Solutions/Alternatives 189

On a recently televised ABC network program, the "20/20" show of January 13, 1995, several severe cases of resident abuse as well as outright theft and thuggery within the nursing home environment were captured on hidden video-tape recorders.[57] Attempts to ask the nursing home proprietors to respond to these cases were often met with little or no comments. These are not isolated incidents, according to the Organization of the California Advocates for Nursing Home Reform.[58] They report a majority of nursing homes in California failed to provide adequate care for the elderly in 1993, causing the death of 16 residents. They also found there are 315 residents who were put in imminent danger of death or serious harm and 1,160 residents' health or safety were jeopardized. Some of the abuses cited include untreated bedsores that led to amputations, untreated broken limbs, drugging or restraining people against their will, and failing to protect them from sexual assaults. These things are happening now,

---

[57]cf. footnote 32.

[58]Weaver, Nancy, *Sacramento Bee*, Aug. 4, 1994, p.1 and 15.

more than seven years after the passage of the OBRA 1987 landmark regulations. What is going on?

Almost all nursing homes operate in a very mediocre fashion. The state inspectors always find the facilities to be "out of standards" with certain regulations. The staff are often grumbling about working conditions and unsanitary environment. The top positions (Administrator and Director of Nursing) and the Certified Nursing Assistants almost always have a nearly 100% annual turnover rate. Stability that we have come to associate with sustained effort and continuity of care is often missing. Why is this the case?

It is certainly true that a disgruntled staff of nurses and CNAs will not and cannot deliver high quality of care to the residents. It is also true that a management/owner who does not care about the welfare of its employees cannot get satisfactory performance from those he hires. In the nursing home industry, the final "product" of the facility is its service to the elderly within its residential confines. When there is a bad product, the responsibility for the problem must reside with the management team first and foremost. The nature of these problems in a nursing home will be discussed. At each stage, the role of the consumer, and the residents and their family members in how they can impact the motives and directions of a facility will be pointed out.

Free Enterprise in the Service Sector

An overwhelming majority of nursing homes operate on a "For Profit" basis. This translates to free enterprise where investors of the facility will try to optimize their profit margin. In the nursing home industry, profit will have to be made off the private-pay residents, those who are approved for Medicare services, and those who are on the federal Medicaid program. Since the Medicaid reimbursement is low, less than $83 per day per resident, and the population of the nursing homes is predominantly Medicaid-supported, one can easily surmise what will be the result.[59] There is a big difference in the operational philosophy between the corporations/owners/ administrative management and the service staff members (nursing department and other ancillary services). Basically, the difference reduces to the following: When the resident census is down, delivery of services is often relegated to a secondary role in comparison with sustaining a level of profit. As a result, if there is money to be saved by utilizing short cuts, the owners/companies will usually take them. While the profit margins are kept at a level the owners like to see, our elderly and frail population who are living in one of these nursing homes take the brunt of the inadequacies. A reduction in services, in the form of barely satisfying the mandates for minimum hours of care per resident, is one avenue taken. The other approach is to hire people at a lower than average wage for corresponding services. The result is that only those workers in a desperate enough situation will assume these positions. They are often ill-prepared to function to give our residents the highest quality of care. Once in a while, when the reference checks become sloppy, even criminals get into the facility to become the caregivers of our loved ones. The main problems in the Nursing Department, by far the largest department within any nursing home, will be identified.

Nursing Department Problems

The nursing staff of a facility are those who are supposed to look out for your loved one's care and rights. They are present 24 hours a day, seven days a week. They are responsible for the total functioning of the facility. Sometimes they are called "jack of all trades" because they are called upon to perform many non-nursing duties. The problems associated with the three categories of nurses are different.

---

[59]Chanecka, Steve, "Nursing homes make case for worthy, needed services", *Senior Spectrum Weekly*, June 10, 1992, p.2.

1. Certified Nursing Assistants (CNAs)

CNAs form the majority of the staff in nursing homes. They are considered the front-line nurses; they do all the daily ADL for the residents. For the bedridden and unconscious residents, they turn them and keep them clean and dry every 2 hours. During mealtime and snack time, they feed those residents who cannot manage to eat by themselves. In a typical nursing home, they each will handle between 10 to 12 residents during the day shift, 15 to 20 during the PM shift, and as many as 25 to 30 residents on night shift. They are often overworked, underpaid, and their efforts are often unappreciated. Yet they are the people who hold an important role in bettering the quality of life of those residents under their immediate care. They make the difference in the resident's daily lives. What the CNA does can make a resident either happy or sad, elated or depressed, laugh or cry. They also have control over whether a resident is hydrated or dehydrated, constipated, diarrhetic or normal functioning. In other words, the resident's life lies precariously in the hands of the CNA. Even though the licensed nurse can give that specific antibiotic to cure an infection, the CNA truly influences the level of comfort, hence the quality of life and care of the resident. They also function as the eyes, the ears, and the nose as well as the hands and feet of the overloaded and overworked LVNs. For those who are truly dedicated to service like that which I just described, I tip my hat to all of them.

a. CNA training - For someone who holds such a major responsibility for the welfare of the residents, one would expect that there would be an extensive training and apprenticeship period. We mentioned before that in order for an individual to obtain a CNA license, he or she must have completed a precertification course consisting of 50 hours of theory and 100 hours of clinical practice. These new students must pass the state certification examination for CNA prior to being able to practice as one. For those CNAs who were hired before this OBRA regulation, they too are required to take a state competency test for CNA. All new CNAs must attend an 8-hour comprehensive orientation session after they are hired before they are allowed to be on the floor for hands-on care of residents. On paper, these guidelines are rigorous. Unfortunately, training of CNAs at the facility level has always been spotty and non-uniform. Sometimes, these students are even pulled out of the classes to staff the floor by the DON due to CNA shortage. This practice is both illegal and disruptive. The ability to produce uniformly well-trained CNAs lies directly with the qualifications of the individual designated to train them, the Direc-tor for Staff Development (DSD).

Every facility has a DSD for personnel orientation and in-service training programs. If she has a state-approved pre-certification program for nursing assistants, then she is also responsible for training and certifying those nursing assistants. She can be an LVN or an RN. If the DSD is not a conscientious instructor, either in teaching the theory portion of the classes, or is not adequately supervising the nursing assistants during their clinical training, then those students are left on the floor to struggle by themselves. They end up having to learn from older CNAs, who may or may not be the best teacher or role model. As a result, even if they pass the certification examination, they may still lack the professionalism, the in-depth education, and the interpersonal relationship skills to handle the residents and their problems.

Basically, an inadequately trained CNA will lack observational skills and caring techniques, as well as good interpersonal relationship mannerisms for this difficult job. They will not realize how important it is to report to the LVNs or the Supervisor if anything out of the routine is happening to any residents under their charge. The authors of the OBRA regulations anticipated this problem, and there is starting to be fewer of the individual facility training programs of non-uniform standard. In their place, more centralized training centers are being considered for the training of nursing assistants. These include intensive three-month and semester sessions at community colleges and career training schools that are coordinated with designated facilities for clinical training.

    b. Resident abuse - When the "20/20" program of January 13, 1995 showed CNAs performing the "slam-dunk" procedure[60] on wheelchair or geri-chair bound residents as a way of putting them to bed, the level of anger and disbelief of the viewer, including me, hit an all-time high. This is overt physical abuse on the defenseless residents. In most facilities, such drastic abuse does not occur. However, resident abuse by CNAs does happen. Because they are constantly in contact with the residents, the CNAs are sometimes blamed for abusing a resident, without knowing the whole story. There could have been a misunderstanding between a resident and the CNA. Sometimes the resident will make up a story of abuse. I have previously cited a few cases where a resident and the CNA did not understand each other, which resulted in confrontations and accusations of abuse. Any confrontation could be construed as verbal or physical abuse, and the accused CNA often has little chance to reply to such a charge. In facilities that are sensitive to complaints of resident abuse, the course of fact-finding and redress is clearly laid out. If after a thorough investigation by the Administration, the staff member is found to be at fault, then that person is automatically terminated without recourse. If the staff member is found to not be at fault, and there was indeed a misunderstanding, appropriate action taken by the facility's administration could include special in-service education and/or a reprimand in the personnel files.

---

[60]The "Slam-dunk" procedure was described on the 20/20 program as one where the CNA rapidly slams on the brakes of the wheelchair. The emaciated resident flips out head first due to this sudden stoppage. The CNA then catches and dunks the resident into his bed, causing emotional trauma and physical injuries.

c. The lot of the CNA - There are, certainly, a number of truly dedicated CNAs in each facility. These individuals are sincerely devoting their lives and work to bettering the lives of the residents. They not only have taken the effort and time to understand the residents under their care, but they are usually willing to be overloaded when the need arises. For these aides their motivation is truly a blessing for the residents. However, no one is immune to politics and back-stabbing in any organization. Too often the one singled out for absorbing the wrath of others is the caring and dedicated CNA who stands alone for principles and compassion and who refuses to become political as a member of a clique. The result is that the good CNA who really cares for the resident's welfare gets kicked out on trumped up charges of ineptness and inadequacy, while the "deadwood", those who spend more time gossiping and manipulating for personal advantage, stay. Even when a bad aide is finally caught for a major infraction against facility rules or policies, the facility is still handicapped. This aide may have allies amongst other aides who will threaten "mass walkout" if disciplinary action is taken against this one individual. Unfortunately for an understaffed facility, this is a significant concern for the management.

d. Staff shortage - Consider the case where a CNA calls in sick. Now the management has three alternatives. To call for backup relief from the facility's own "On-Call" list is the most expedient option. A second choice is to contact a Nursing Registry Service for temporary replacement. The third option is simply to leave the slot open and force the few CNAs on duty to take up an even heavier load. Few facilities have a trustworthy and reliable relief pool of CNAs, and the management usually does not like to use Registry CNAs because Registry personnel costs the facility twice that of the regular employee. Furthermore, often the non-attached status of the Registry personnel leads to a "don't care" attitude. Without adequate backup personnel to substitute in case of sickness, emergencies or unexcused absence, the Nursing Department often must resort to loading the extra residents on the available CNAs. This obviously causes dissension when the situation happens too frequently. If there is no appreciation shown by the Administration, morale goes down, and consequently the level of care goes down. After a while, those assistants who are truly dedicated get burnt out and leave.

e. *The revolving door policy* - Disciplinary action for serious offenses against a resident usually can be taken without too much fear of local insurrection. However, on the matter of personnel action, application of disciplinary action becomes quite non uniform. A common situation is one where certain CNAs make it a habit of calling in sick for the weekend, or calling in sick for Monday after a weekend off. The facility's options for disciplinary action are limited. CNAs have no fear of losing their jobs, because they know they can get another job easily in a different facility on the same day they are fired from the first facility. They know the biggest hurdle for the hiring facility is being able to get an accurate reference check. All facilities are afraid of law suits. The only information the former facility gives out is the day he is hired and the day he left. Sometimes inadvertently a person with a criminal record such as theft, assault and battery, or a known sex offender slips through the reference checks, and gets a job working in one of these facilities. In California, there is a state registry where you can check for a CNA's criminal record. There should be similar registry in all other states.

f. *Incompatibility factor* - The SNF residential population is overwhelmingly female. Often the ratio of female residents to male residents can be as high as four to one, and most of them are well into their 80s or older. On the other hand, the CNAs are often teenagers, ethnic minorities and single parents. Nowadays, there are more and more males entering this field as nursing assistants. The combination of the age difference and in the case of a male CNA working with female residents, the gender difference can make for some very trying times for all. Some young male assistants probably have never taken care of elderly female residents in their whole life. Consequently they may lack full understanding of the physical as well as the psychological needs of these residents. Other assistants with distinctively different cultural backgrounds often allow their own prejudices toward the elderly to be very transparent. Yet they are in that position to be the front-line caregiver to the same elderly residents, who sometimes can be very demanding. It is easy to see that if the staff in-service education and precertification classes were inadequately taught, physical abuses and neglect will occur as a result of misunderstandings and temper flare-ups.

Incompatibility comes in another form also. The CNAs are one of the lowest paid service employees anywhere. Their wages are only marginally higher than the minimum wages. The average hourly salary for CNAs in the State of California is about $6.50. At that kind of wage, the CNA often feels alienated and disenfranchised. Such feelings are not conducive to dedication toward the job. There is no caring attitude. To some it is only a job that they must have for survival or to satisfy the state welfare department's rules regarding work.

Solutions:

1. The standard and qualification of the DSD must be raised. The total job description for the DSD must be one that focuses more on compassionate bedside nursing care. The CNAs, irrespective of their ethnic and cultural background or age, must be taught the uniform application of nursing care procedures as well as how to develop a keen sense of nursing observation. The DSD must be on the floor to provide skill training guidance at all times. He should be abreast with the newest problems and solutions and constantly be educating the CNAs through in-service classes.

2. Since the CNAs do play an absolutely essential role in the care of the residents, the Administration must treat

them with the proper type of respect. Not only should there be well-established guidelines for wage increases to something substantially above the minimum wage, there must be a daily indication of appreciation for the effort the CNAs provide, and for their jobs well done. The DON and Nursing Supervisor, along with the Administrator must openly praise those individuals for superior performance of jobs and administrate discrete and judicious punishment for those in the wrong.

3. The Nursing Department should develop an "on-call" list or a back-up system so that when staffing shortage arises, the names on this list can be called upon with reliability. It is possible that some CNAs would jump at the chance to carry on an extra shift for 1.5 times the normal wages. It is also possible to pay on-call CNAs a fraction of their normal wage just to remain on that list actively.

4. Because the CNA is required to carry out strenuous physical work, some form of endurance test may be called upon prior to hiring. This test may be able to weed out those who cannot maintain the level of endurance for the job at hand. In this manner, excessive sickness, injury and workman's compensation times can all be kept to a minimum.

5. Some form of procedure for disciplinary action needs to be established to discourage unexcused absences. Facilities should organize on a statewide level to establish general and uniform guidelines regarding disciplinary action and reference checks. Threats and intimidation by employees and employers alike cannot be tolerated. Statewide arbitration board hearing procedures of employee grievances should be made available in all cases.

2. Licensed Vocational Nurses (LVN)

LVNs make up the largest component of the supervisory team among the licensed nursing personnel. They are each responsible for supervising the CNAs on their shift as well as the welfare of between 30 to 60 residents. They are in charge of passing medications, a process that is usually time-consuming due to the fact most residents take multiple medications. Each resident needs to be sought out, because they often are not in their rooms. Sometimes the residents refuse to take the medication, and then the nurse must chart this fact and what actions were taken. The interval between medication passes is very short. This is one of the reasons why you see these nurses always behind the carts. If there is no treatment nurse that day, LVNs also have to do treatments. They are also called upon to assume the dining room monitoring duties during mealtimes. Furthermore, they need to write 3 to 4 weekly summaries on residents under their charge in order to cover the entire population on a monthly basis. If any of the residents are on antibiotics for an infection, had a fall, or had any unusual changes in physical or mental condition, they have to chart on them every shift. This can take up 2 to 3 hours out of the 8-hour period. The PM and night shift LVNs also have to be responsible for the accuracy of the monthly updated Physician's Medical Sheet (PMR). If there is an epidemic, the load of charting goes even higher. This leaves very little time to supervise the CNAs. If the Nursing Supervisor is willing to write the weekly summaries for her, then it will relieve some of her load. It is no wonder the nurses are dead tired and frustrated at the end of each shift. For all this work, their efforts are often not appreciated by the family members and not by the Administration at all. If they stay longer to complete the required work, there is not only no compensation either in days off or in overtime, there is often admonishment that overtime implies incompetence.

Just as in the case of the CNAs, even among the few LVNs on duty, there is "office politics". Getting along with the CNAs is a necessity for survival. Being able to work with other LVNs helps also to ease the load since cooperation can mean helping each other in time of need. The transition between shifts is often a point of communication breakdown if the nurses do not get along well. Missed information transmittal could mean necessary care is overlooked.

Unfortunately, some of the most dedicated, caring, and energetic licensed nurses who concentrate their efforts on giving the best of care to the residents are the first ones to get in trouble with the Administration. Why? Because they possess too much knowledge about the right way to do things, and they tend to be more precise in following the regulations. They also want to give residents autonomy or more free choice in their daily care, which may not fit in well with the facility's task-oriented timelines. They challenge the budget-minded administration/owner on supplies and personnel deficits. As a result, they are singled out as trouble-makers. Once singled out, all it takes is a minor complaint or incident from any staff, and the Administration will conjure up an excuse to terminate that employee. The forum for rebuttal of charges differs from facility to facility. The accused has no place to turn to for help, and often the Director of Nursing is under direct orders to terminate that staff member no matter what she says to the contrary in her defense. If the DON does not comply with management's wishes, her own job is on the line also.

Solutions:

1. We are unable to take human nature out for special redress, for we are all political animals to some extent. What can be done is to take some of the drudgery out of the work. For the LVNs who are both medical and treatment nurses, the most obvious thing to omit from their job duties are the weekly summaries that they must write. If we consider the nursing home to be a "home" for most of the residents, we understand that their conditions are chronic, not acute. What is the purpose of writing or copying weekly summaries over and over again? No new information is gained by these summaries, but valuable resident care time is lost. I propose that documentation should be made only upon reported changes of conditions. This is a point where you as the consumer can have an impact. Bring up this point at the Family Council meeting. Ask the DON and Administrator to

take a lead and start questioning the mandated policies regarding the weekly summary sheets. You should be able to let your Congressmen and Senators know that it is far more impor-tant to have quality service than immaculate bookkeeping.

2. Facilities must establish, according to their own policies, an equitable and judicious process to redress grievances, including unjustified termination. It may not be too much of a stretch of the imagination to involve the Family Council members in these deliberations, either as jury or observers. Heavy-handed and unilateral actions taken by some powerful administrative personnel could be ameliorated by the mere presence of an outside observer. Who better than the residents and their family members would have a stake in the retaining of a dedicated nurse about to be drummed out by political savagery?

3. Supervisors

Supervisors are all Registered Nurses (RNs). They handle all the admissions, assess the residents' change of conditions, call the physicians, coordinate MDS, hold care-plan conference meetings, and interact with families and various departments. It is the sole duty of the Nursing Supervisor to monitor the care and the duties of all the nursing staff on the floor. She must keep the Director of Nursing appraised and up-to-date on all the problems that occur daily. She is considered the right-hand of the DON. If the Supervisor is negligent and incompetent in her assessment skills and does not keep the DON apprised, and if the hands of the DON are tied in her attempts to discipline that Supervisor, then the DON simply functions as a "figurehead" or a "scapegoat". The problems inherent to the job of Nursing Supervisor are that sometimes the individuals do not know the federal and state regulations or the Medicare guidelines thoroughly themselves. If the facility does not belong to some sort of long-term care facilities organization, all pertin-ent and important new information is not transmitted to the staff. The leadership role of the Supervisor weakens with the lack of information, and this weakness filters downward to project a weak facility image.

Solution: Each facility has only a few Nursing Supervisors. Since the individual with the title of Supervisor is to be considered the assistant to the Director of Nursing, the DON should have a major say in the type of individual he/she wants for the Supervisor. Qualifications for the Supervisor, besides being self-motivated and knowledgeable in regulations, must include the ability to work with the pharmacy consultant. Earlier I had discussed one of the major problem of SNF is the over-abundance of multiple drug usage by residents. A major responsibility of the Supervisor is to be knowledgeable in the field of drug interaction so as to be able to discuss methods of reducing drugs. She will then have to be poised enough to discuss with the physicians prescribing a reduction. If successful, this will in turn decrease the amount of time the LVNs use to administer medications. The reduced level of medication could well benefit the resident's total well-being. As in all service-client situations, the advisory input of the client in the choosing of the Supervisor could be helpful. Currently, the residents have no voice in whom they want for leading the care team. They always find out the situation after the fact. I propose an advisory committee composed of members from the Resident or Family Councils be established to assist the DON in choosing the Nursing Supervisor.

4. Director of Nursing (DON)

The DON is the one who oversees all functions of the Nursing Department. The DON is ultimately responsible for any and all deficiencies committed by the nursing staff. On the surface, this seems to be reasonable, since the DON is in principle in charge of all the Nursing Department's affairs. Actually, she is often hindered in carrying out her responsibilities by a Supervisor who fails to keep her abreast on the day-to-day nursing department affairs. Since "the buck (in the nursing department) stops here", she must be held responsible for all of the short-comings of the department. As a result, turn-over at this level is extremely high, and that is a significant problem. Because this mid-level management position is unstable, and each new DON inherits all of the unsolved problems of her predecessors, whenever there is a change in the DON, the entire nursing staff is frustrated and tense. The gap of communication widens and the trust factor diminishes with a new DON, and valuable time is lost until everybody adjusts to this new person. In some facilities, this position does not stabilize for months at a time. Of course, without a stable, knowledgeable DON whose goal is to strive for a high quality of life and care for the residents, the residents and the facility both suffer in the long run. What is the cause for this instability at the top?

a. Staffing inadequacies - The DON is responsible for fully staffing the nursing needs of the facility. Current regulations call for an average of 3.0 care hours per resident per 24-hour day. In most facilities, this is barely attained if the full staff in present. If someone calls in sick, a juggling act begins. This is particularly acute in facilities with less than 50 beds. In those facilities, the Administration just wants one RN on duty; this RN is the DON and act as the Supervisor/charge nurse. If one of her LVNs calls in sick, and she cannot find a replacement from her own facility, she is not normally allowed to call a Nurses' Registry for temporary help. Instead, she has to work on the floor as a charge nurse. How long do you think this individual can last, especially without the Administrator's or owner's support? No nurse is stupid enough to stay there long under these working conditions.

b. Consultant pressure - Besides the normal problems of staffing and disciplining, the DON also has to deal with outside consultant pressure. Consultants are contracted by the Administration to come into the facility on a monthly basis to review the status of the Nursing Department. Because she is contracted by the Administrator, she feels an obligation to report only to that person. As a result, the consultant often looks upon the DON as a challenge, and vice versa, i.e., the DON thinks of the consultant as a meddler. Often, communication breaks down between these two. However, the DON needs consultants to provide new ideas to solve the identified problems that are in critical need of assistance. The DON does not need a rehash of the well-known shortcomings. Unfortunately many of the consultants are not there to help they often make matters worse. If the DON challenges the consultant's authority or input, her position is put in jeopardy. She has to comply with several bosses instead of one. Each one has his own ideas of how to do the work, even if it means following them without any consideration of her own facility's policies or procedures. In the end, if the facility is in trouble, her license is on the line and not that of the consultant's. After all the hooplas the persons who suffer the most are the poor, vulnerable residents. They are hopelessly and helplessly trapped in this unsettling environment. They have no idea what is going on in their facility, which is considered their home. You should ask: Where are their rights to have a stable environment for a home? Who looks out for their total welfare if the nursing staff cannot?

c. Office politics - At the department heads level, office politics can be even more vicious. Even though the DON heads by far the largest department within a facility, she is ranked equal to the heads of other departments such as the laundry or house-keeping units. In most facilities, she is not even directly in charge of the DSD's activities. Often staff members and the owner are personal friends. Hence favoritism enters. Given such an environment, there is a great deal of office politics and back-stabbing among various department head personnel. The DON will have to fit into that small clique of "most favored department heads" in order to survive. In most cases, survival as the DON does not depend on dedication, know-ledge, skills or hard work. The motto seems to be, "If you fit in, no matter how incompetent you are, no one can touch you, and you can do no wrong. You are protected by the mother hen."

Example: A Supervisor did an initial assessment of a newly admitted resident and reported that there were no medical complications with this person. When the Director of Nursing visited the new resident as a part of the welcoming visit on the same day of admission, the resident complained that her heel hurts. Upon taking her socks off, the DON found the area to be red and tender to the touch. She asked the resident why she did not tell the admissions nurse about this condition. Her reply was that this admitting nurse did not care to listen to her and never took the socks off for an examination. The DON immediately notified the Charge Nurse. The physician was also called and treatment orders were received. The wound healed without complication in a few days. The DON brought her concern about the Supervisor to the Administrator and suggested appropriate disciplinary action be taken. Promises were made, but nothing happened.

Solutions:

1. The DON should be placed in a position above all other department heads. She does not need to be in a position to supervise other department heads, and she should not have to be accountable to them in any manner. Her immediate superior should only be the Administrator.

2. Because of the close ties between nurse training and in-service education, the DSD must be a member of the nursing education team, accountable to the DON for what and how she teaches, not to the Administrator.

3. It should be made clear that consultants to the facility are there to help resolve problems that already existed, as well as for quality assessment. The most import-ant person who the consultant should work with must be the

DON. Only the Administrator can make that fact clear to the consultant before any consultation reports are written.

4. The DON should be given a working budget within which she is free to operate as she sees fit for attaining the highest level of care for all the residents. The choice of using various outside personnel or specific inside personnel should be entirely her decision. The Administrator should not interfere in any of these internal Nursing Department affairs. In like manner, disciplinary actions within the Nursing Department should be entirely the pervue of the DON, with no Administration interference, but with total Administrative support.

5. For the DON to gain the trust of and open communication lines with her staff, she must show that she is not afraid to get her own hands dirty. She should be able and willing to help anyone in the Nursing Department "in a pinch". Calling a physician or emptying a bedpan should be as familiar to her as writing a report of carrying out a disciplinary action.

6. When a facility gets continually poor state inspectors' reviews, the owners of the corporation should investigate thoroughly the source of trouble. Sometimes the problem does not lie with either the Administrator or the Director of Nursing; each level of front-line nursing practice may be a potential source of non-compliance. The Supervisor for one, being the individual who has the day-to-day responsibility of keeping the floors deficiency-free, needs to be accountable. Objective evaluation of all personnel is absolutely essential.

The problems which I have pointed out in the Nursing Department all focus on one point: even though there is the stated common goal of providing the highest level of quality care for the residents, there is little or no teamwork among the staff. The administration wants profits the state wants highest quality of life and care for all the residents. The licensed nurses and CNAs are overworked, underpaid and unappreciated for their effort. To overhaul the problems that exist in these facilities, I believe that the time is ripe for the consumers, the residents and their families, to stand together and declare that they will not be short-changed in having the highest quality of care. By confronting the entire nursing home industry, by making the facilities responsible for all of their actions, and by policing the facilities as intelligent citizens, the industry will be forced to change. The nursing home industry must be made more humane and more responsible.

Physicians:

Often, physicians responsible for residents in a long-term care facility do not demonstrate good leadership for the staff to follow. They are often frustrated when it comes to caring for the long-term care residents. They often carry an attitude of not being overly concerned in the caring for these elderly. The average time a doctor spends in the facility is approximately 20 minutes a month signing charts and saying hello to the residents. Some of them do not even recognize their own patients. They do not know what the condition is of their patients. The principal reason for this is that they were trained to cure patients. In the case of the elderly, cure is often temporary. Eventual debilitation, deterioration, dehumanization and demise are difficult concepts for these physicians to accept and cope with. As a result, their response time to the calls from the nurses in the facility who notice a change of condition of a resident is often long or not at all. This in turn frustrates the concerned nurses and certainly is not in the best interest or welfare of the residents. Sometimes the physicians cannot handle dying residents and their eventual deaths because they take deaths as personal defeats.

Solution: We must educate the physicians that it is all right to let go, to be proud that he contributed to the comfort and care of the resident who is at his last stage of life. With regard to physicians not responding to nurses' calls, or being curt in their response, often this is the nurses' own fault. When poorly trained nurses show a lack of judgment, knowledge, or skills to think for themselves, they will call the physician for unimportant orders frequently and at odd hours. This frustrates the busy physician. To resolve this dilemma, the nurses should be thoroughly prepared for intelligent assessment before calling the physician.

General solutions/alternatives:

1. Increase the (generally) very low wages for entering CNAs. Pay each new employee based upon his experience, attitude, and personality. Have a merit system in place for all employees who have passed their probationary period.

2. Give fringe benefits earlier such as comprehensive health care after 30 days of employment instead of the usual waiting period of three months. The DON should be able to assess a dedicated, caring staff member immediately without any doubts or hesitation.

3. Change hiring practices to create joy and vitality. Preference should be placed on individuals with dedication, creativity and initiative. Provide flexibility in the scheduling of staff personnel so that those individuals with the desirable qualities can benefit from the needed flexibility.

4. Set up a promotional ladder as part of a positive reinforcement system. Reward the truly excellent staff with upward mobility through education. Offer to send those to nursing school with free tuition and a guaranteed higher level position waiting for them upon their return.

5. The licensed nurses should also be continuously learning and increasing their level of nursing skills in the nursing home environment. In-depth education programs should be available for them to be more aware of significant changes in resident conditions, particularly with respect to behavior and mental conditions. In-services should also be conducted on up-to-date and efficient charting methods so that information is complete, yet succinct. All staff members must be kept abreast of the newest federal and state

regulations by regular meetings that include the Administrator and the DON.

6. Have a comprehensive 16-hour orientation program for all new staff members before allowing them to be on the floor for hands-on care of residents. If needed, allow 2 to 3 extra orientation days for a new CNA to work with another senior CNA on a one-to-one basis.

7. Have a child care center in the facility to alleviate two things:) For the staff with children, it relieves the need to search for a close-by, reliable day-care setting. ii) For the residents, a child care center can relieve boredom and give them a constructive outlet for their pent-up energy. Watching the imagination and energy of children at play can renew even the eldest resident's spirit. The child so cared will also benefit by having proxy grandparents to instill moral and ethical values to them. Charging a minimal fee for the usage of this facility should present no problem.

8. The Administration (owner/corporation head-quarters) should promote a positive attitude, provide a good working environment, show support, care and appreciation for the quality staff, and have an open line of communication with the staff.

9. The last recommendation involves you and your loved one and may be the most important point to retain good staff in your facility. The best thing you and your loved one can do to assist the nurses is not to disturb them by calling the facility between the hours of 8 to 10 AM, 1 to 2 PM, and 4 to 6 PM. The reason is that every time you are calling about your loved one's condition, the nurse must stop her medication pass, lock the medication cart, and run to the nurse's station to answer the phone. This consumes her already limited medication pass time.

In summary, residents will always receive poor quality of care so long as there is inadequate training of the CNAs and deficient knowledge of the licensed nurses. I have pointed out some of the other problems in the nursing home that will be detrimental to the residents. Currently, there is little or no teamwork concept in this very complex health delivery system. The CNAs receive little or no supervision from the licensed nurses, and the licensed nurses receive little in-service education of significance. Communication between shifts is poor and inadequate for complete transfer of information about residents. All of the staff in the nursing facilities are overloaded, overworked, and underpaid. On the other hand, the management expects completed work with little or no overtime. In the meantime, the state wants the facility to be citation-free in an era where the required amount of paperwork makes it impossible for the nurses to succeed. There needs to be a way for the corporation/owner/Administrator to realize that changing its way of managing the staff will improve the morale of the employees and the care of the residents. They need to go to bat for their employees. When the residents and families see this side of the management, they will join in the effort to impress upon legislators and regulators the importance of streamlining the bureaucracy of paper shuffling. It is only by those means that the profit derived from operating this type of enterprise can be considered fulfilling and rewarding.

One final thought on how you the consumer can help to strengthen this service industry. The topic is the level of Medicaid reimbursement for the facility. At the present time, a resident who has to be cared for around the clock (room, board, and nursing care) in a nursing home facility is being reimbursed by Medicaid at a daily "room rate" less than that of a motel room. Where are the priorities?

ADDENDUM[61]

On August 28, 1992, HCFA published a Notice of Proposed Rule-making (57 **Fed. Reg.** 39278) regarding changes of OBRA 87 designed to ensure improvements in nursing home care. After this public announcement, the agency received nearly 28,000 public comments on various issues dealing with how to improve the care of residents in these nursing homes. The main problems that were perceived in OBRA 87 are two-fold. First of all, introduction of the MDS and the RAI made it look as if the inspectors are focusing more heavily on paperwork compliance rather than actual quality of care of the residents. Secondly, there are facilities that will force an overload of personnel just prior to state inspection, improving the quality of care just enough during the few short weeks around the time of inspection to rate a "pass", only to fall again after the facility had passed the inspection. These facilities are called the "yo-yo" facilities. In effect, these facilities are really in "substantial non-compliance" during much of the year, as judged by the number of complaints filed against them. In its new guidelines announced on November 10, 1994, HCFA set forth its final regulations on how to enforce and interpret the law (OBRA 94). This final version of the law took effect on July 1, 1995. The goals of the new enforcement regulations are:

1. to motivate facilities to remain in constant "substantial compliance", and to discourage "yo-yo" compliance,
2. to ensure equitable and consistent enforcement,
3. to link appropriate remedy to deficiencies, and
4. to create no unnecessary process.

---

[61]On June 29 and 30, 1995, the author attended an informational workshop pertaining to the newest OBRA (1994) guidelines on nursing home regulation. This was a program put forth by the California Association of Health Facilities, in Sacramento, CA.

The guidelines of OBRA 94 encourage the state inspectors to focus their attention on the outcome of the care and not on paperwork. Inspectors are asked to observe the residents themselves while in a particular facility. Instead of certifying that MDS and RAI are logically consistent, they want to see if the tasks set forth by the MDS are indeed carried out. This is accomplished by looking at the physical and mental condition of the residents. During the annual inspection, state inspectors must do their own observations. Also during their stay inspectors interview staff and residents several times a day. They will interview the residents regarding quality of care and quality of life. They will observe and question CNAs on the duties and their front-line observations of resident conditions. They will take note to see if reported changes of conditions are being transmitted to nursing personnel and written plans of action are being followed through by all.

In remedying yo-yo facilities, the new regulations are extremely hard on them. First of all, facilities are categorized into two types: either it is a good performer facility, in constant "substantial compliance" with the rules, in which case little or no remedy will be imposed, or it is a poor performer, which is the characteristic described as a yo-yo facility. The good providers will be given a reasonable time to correct minor, usually non-life-threatening deficiencies. On the other hand, if the facility is a poor performer, that is, it is in continuous yo-yo non-compliance, it will have no grace period to correct the deficiencies before an enforcement remedy is imposed. Such enforcement remedy can result in civil money penalties or worse. There is a matrix categorizing the scope and severity of the infraction for the state inspectors to follow (See Table). This matrix consists of four levels of severity for substandard quality in the care, specifically dealing with deficiencies in resident behavior and facility practice, and the resultant quality of life and quality of care.

MATRIX OF VIOLATIONS AND REMEDIES

Severity level   **Plan of Action**

	ISOLATED	PATTERN	WIDE-SPREAD
Immediate jeopardy to resident health or safety	Required: #3 Optional: #2 Optional: #1	Required: #3 Optional: #2 Optional: #1	Required: #3 Optional: #2 Optional: #1
Actual harm that is not immediate jeopardy	Required: #2 Optional: #1	Required: #2 Optional: #1	Required: #2 Optional: #1 Optional: temporary mgmt.
No actual harm with potential for more than minimal harm (not of immediate jeopardy)	Required: #1 Optional: #2	Required: #1 Optional: #2	Required: #2 Optional: #1
No actual harm with potential for minimal harm	No remedies. Commitment to correct.		

#1, #2, AND #3 ARE CATEGORIES OF REMEDIES

(See below in text)

TABLE

The four levels of severity are:

1. immediate jeopardy to residents' health and safety,
2. actual harm that is not of immediate jeopardy,
3. no actual harm but with potential for more than minimal harm that is not immediate jeopardy,
4. no actual harm with potential for minimal harm.

Each level of severity has a specified remedy category based on the scope of violation.

The three scopes are:

1. is it an isolated situation?
2. is it developing into a pattern?
3. is it already a widespread situation in this facility?

At the end of their survey, the inspectors will have a team conference with their own supervisor and then write up the report. Once the penalty or remedy is imposed, the facility cannot challenge the remedy, but it can still have one hearing under either federal or state procedure to dispute the deficiencies to a lower level of severity if there are substantial facts backing up such claims.

The main focus for the inspectors will be on those facilities with the most problems in those problem areas using data gathered off-site as well as on-site. The investigator can impose various remedies to the facility according to the scope and severity of the deficiency. The state inspectors can impose the following categories of remedies:

Category 1 - Directed plan of correction and/or directed inservice training, either of which can be monitored by the state;

Category 2 - Denial of payment for new admissions, denial of payment for all individuals, imposed by HCFA, or civil money penalties from $50 to $3,000 per day;

Category 3 - Temporary management by the state or termination and closure where the residents are then transferred from the facility for emergency situations. Civil money penalties from $3,001 to $10,000 per day may be imposed as an option in this category.

In order to try to bring a substandard facility up to standard, HCFA will allow the state inspectors to assist the facility. They can serve as technical information transfer officers assigned to that facility; they will provide the facility alternative and creative methods to meet the quality of life and quality of care of residents. Because of this additional relentless pursuit by the state mandated by HCFA, facility owners should take note that life can be much more pleasant if his/her facility is in "substantial compliance". The "catch up and fix-it-up" schemes practiced by the poor facilities will not survive under these new enforcement guidelines. The nursing home residents are finally truly being protected by the new public law. The public, particularly those who have the need to choose a good nursing home for their loved ones, can easily be guided by this matrix as to where a particular facility fits. With the new enforcement mandated by HCFA, the federal government, the states and the providers will be working closely together toward the same goal for all the residents: to attain or to maintain the highest practical level of function in physical, emotional, spiritual and psychosocial well-being. In due time, the only facilities left running should be those that maintain substantial compliance.

BIBLIOGRAPHY

Acker, Susan, Workshop on Reducing the Use of Chemical Restraints in Nursing Homes, Serial No. 102-6, U.S. Government Printing Office, 1991, p.51.

Ambrogi, D.M., Nursing Home Admissions: Problematic Process and Agreements, *Generations*, Supplement, 1990, pp.72-74.

Beers, M.H., Fingold, S.F., Ouslander, J.G., Reuben, D.B., Morganstern, H. and Beck, J.C., Characteristics and Quality of Prescribing by Doctors Practicing in Nursing Homes, *J. Am. Geriatrics Soc.*, 41: 1993, pp.802-807.

Birren, J.E., Lubben, J.E., Rowe, J.C. and Deutchman, D.E., The Concept and Measurement of Quality of Life in the Frail Elderly. Academic Press, Inc., San Diego, 1991.

Blakeslee, Jill, Untie the Elderly, *Am. J. Nursing*, June,1988, pp.833-834.

Blazer, Dan & Siegler, Ilene C., A Family Approach to Health Care of the Elderly, Addison-Wesley Publishing Co., Menlo Park, 1984.

Brannon, Diane & Smyer, Michael A., Who Will Provide Long-Term Care in the Future?, *Generations* , Spring, 1990, pp.64-67.

Browne, Colette and Onzuka-Anderson, Roberta, Our Aging parents: A Practical Guide to Eldercare, University of Hawaii Press, Honolulu, 1985.

Budish, Armond D., Avoiding the Medicaid Trap: How to Beat the Catastrophic Costs of Nursing Home Care, Henry Holt and Co. New York, 1994.

Burger, Sarah, Detrimental effects of physical and chemical restraints on residents. National Center for State Long Term Care Ombudsman Resources,1989, pp.57-61.

Burger, Sarah Geeene, Improving the Quality of Care, *The American Nurse,* July/August, 1993.

Cadieux, Roger J., M.D., Geriatric psychopharmacology: The use of psychotropic drugs. In *Psychotropic Drugs and the Elderly Patient,* San Francisco Institute on Aging.,1992, pp.3-14.

California Department of Aging, Questions and Answers on the California Partnership for Long-Term Care, CDA-HICAP publication.

California Department of Aging, Taking Care of Tomorrow: A Consumer's Guide to Long-Term Care, CDA publication.

Carrot, Marion, Symposium on Untie the Elderly: Quality Care without Restraints, Serial No. 101-H, U.S. Government Printing Office, 1990, p.42.

Chanecka, Steve, "Nursing homes make case for worthy, needed services", *Senior Spectrum Weekly,* June 10, 1992, p.2.

Cheren, Connie, Symposium on Untie the Elderly: Quality Care without Restraints, Serial No. 101-H, U.S. Government Printing Office, 1990, p.61.

Committee on Nursing Home Regulation, Institute of Medicine, Improving the Quality of Care in Nursing Homes, National Academy Press, Washington, D.C., 1986, Chapters 1,2, and Appendix A: "History of Federal Nursing Home Regulation".

Coronado, Ramon, "Nursing home sued over use of mind-altering drugs". *Sacramento Bee,* Dec. 10, 1993, p.B4

Crier, Catherine, in a segment of the *20/20* program, ABC Network, January 13, 1995.

Doctors can help patients without drug coverage get free prescriptions, Secure Retirement Official publication of the National Committee to Preserve Social Security and Medicare.

Dunkle, Ruth E. and Wykle, May L., Decision Making in Long- Term Care: Factors in Planning. Springer Publishing Co., NY., 1988.

Edinberg, Mark A., Talking with Your Aging Parents, Shambhala Publications, Inc., Boston, 1987.

Elon, Rebecca, M.D., Workshop on Reducing the Use of Chemical Restraints in Nursing Homes, Serial No. 102-6, U.S. Government Printing Office, 1991, pp16-21.

Evans, Lois, & Strumph, Neville E., Tying down the elderly, *J. Am. Geriatric Society*, 37: 1989, pp.65-74.

Farber, Farley Wade, Symposium on Untie the Elderly: Quality Care without Restraints, Serial No. 101-H, U.S. Government Printing Office, 1990, p.38.

Fizel, J.L. and Nunnikhoven, T.S., The Efficiency of Nursing Home Chains, *Applied Economics*, 25: 1993, pp.49-55.

Fleck, Barbara, Modern rest homes have new image. *Daily Democrat*, The, Woodland, CA, June 25, 1995, p.1.

Fox, Nancy, You, Your Parents, and the Nursing Home, Geriatric Press, Inc., Bend OR, 1982.

Garrard, Judith, et al., Evaluation of Neuroleptic drug use by nursing home elderly under proposed Medicare and Medicaid regulations. *J. Am. Med. Assn.* 265:1991, pp.463-467.

Gillogly, Barbara, California Certified Nursing Assistant's Course, Quality Care Health Foundation, 1988.

Grant, Keith, Symposium on Untie the Elderly: Quality Care without Restraints, Serial No. 101-H, U.S. Government Printing Office, 1990, p.6.

Grossberg, G.T., M.D., et al., Psychiatric Problems in the Nursing Home, *J. Am. Geriatrics Soc.* 38: 1990, pp.907-917.

Guide to Choosing a Nursing Home, HCFA-US DHHS

Heinz, Hon. John, Senator, Pennsylvania. In opening statement of the Special Committee on Aging, U.S. Senate, Symposium on Untie the Elderly: Quality Care without Restraints, Serial No. 101-H, 1990, p.1.

Hofland, G.F. and David, D., Autonomy and Long-Term Care Practice: Conclusions and Next Steps, *Generations*, Supplement ,1990, pp.91-94.

Jennings, Christopher, Symposium on Untie the Elderly: Quality Care without Restraints, Serial No. 101-H, U.S. Government Printing Office, 1990, p.3.

Johnson, Colleen L., and Grant, Leslie A., The Nursing Home in American Society, The Johns Hopkins University Press, Baltimore, 1985.

Kane, R.A., Freeman, I.C., Caplan, A.L., Aroskar, M.A. and Urv-Wong, E. K., Everyday Autonomy in Nursing Homes, Generations, Supplement, 1990, pp.69-71.

Kane, R.L., Ouslander, J.G. & Abrass, I.B., Essentials of Clinical Geriatrics, McGraw-Hill Book Co., NY, 1984.

Kane, R.S., Factors Affecting Physician Participation in Nursing Home Care, J. Am. Geriatrics Soc., 41: 1993, pp.1000-1003.

Kapp, Marshall B., Symposium on Untie the Elderly: Quality Care without Restraints, Serial No. 101-H, U.S. Government Printing Office, 1990, p.28-29.

Klitch, Beth A., Workshop on Reducing the Use of Chemical Restraints in Nursing Homes, Serial No. 102-6, U.S. Government Printing Office, 1991, p.46

Lang, Daphne M., Dollars & Sense, Comptalk, I am invincible...I think.Senior Magazine - The Capitol City Edition, Feb. 1994, p.16.

Lang, Daphne M., Dollars & Sense, Comptalk, You really can take it with you! Part I and II, Senior Magazine , The Capitol City Edition, July and September 1994, p.23.

Linkletter, Art, Old Age is Not For Sissies, L'Audace Inc., 1988.

Lippincott Manual of Nursing Practice, The, 4th Edition, J. B. Lipponcott Co., 1986, p.896.

Long Term Care Survey, The, American Health Care Association, Washington, D.C., 1992.

Long, Zofia, Workshop on Reducing the Use of Chemical Restraints in Nursing Homes, Serial No. 102-6, U.S. Government Printing Office, 1991, p11.

Lynn, Joanne, MD.,Symposium on <u>Untie the Elderly: Quality Care without Restraints</u>, Serial No. 101-H, U.S. Government Printing Office, 1990, p.33.

Malone, M.L., Thompson, L. and Goodwin, J.S., Aggressive Behaviors among the Institutionalized Elderly, *J. Am. Geriatrics Soc.*, 41: 1993, pp.853-856.

Manning, Doug, <u>When Love Gets Tough: The Nursing Home Dilemma</u>, Harper & Row, Publishers, San Francisco, 1990.

McConnell, Stephen, Who Cares about Long-Term Care? *Generations*, Spring, 1990, pp.15-18.

McKenna, Kathleen Z., Activists give state poor marks on nursing homes.*Sacramento Bee*, Aug. 5, 1993, p.A3

Medicare Handbook, The, U.S. Department of Health and Human Services Health Care Financing Administration,1992, 1993 and 1994.

Mettler, David, Symposium on <u>Untie the Elderly: Quality Care without Restraints</u>, Serial No. 101-H, U.S. Government Printing Office, 1990, p.22.

Mikulencak, Mandy, "The Graying of America - Changing What Nurses Need to Know". *The American Nurse*, July/Aug. 1993, p.12.

Mitchell-Petersen, Lynne, Symposium on <u>Untie the Elderly: Quality Care without Restraints</u>, Serial No. 101-H, U.S. Government Printing Office, 1990, 50.

Morris, J.N., Hawes, C., Murphy, K., Nonemaker, S., Phillips, C., Fries, B.E. & Mor, V., <u>Resident Assessment Instrument Training Manual and Resource Guide</u>, Eliot Press, Natick, MA, 1991.

Mount, Jeanine, Workshop on <u>Reducing the Use of Chemical Restraints in Nursing Homes</u>, Serial No. 102-6, U.S. Government Printing Office, 1991, p.21.

Murphy, D.J., Burrows, D., Santilli, S., Kemp, A.W., Tenner, S., Kreling, B. and Teno, J., The Influence of the Probability of Survival on Patients' Preferences Regarding Cardiopulmonary Resuscitation, *New England J. Medicine*, 330: 1994, pp.545-549.

Murphy, D.J., Can We Set Futile Care Policies? Institutional and Systemic Challenges, *J. Am. Geriatrics Soc.*, 41: 1994, pp.890-893.

Nick, Susan, LTC, Choice for Geriatric Residents. *J. of Gerontological Nursing*, 18:1992, pp.11-18 .

OBRA Making it Work: A Surveyor's Study Guide to Antipsychotic Drug Use in Nursing Homes, Am. Health Care Association, 1992.

Olsen, C.G., Ouslander, J.G., Singer, K. and Zimmer, J.G., Keeping nursing home residents out of the hospital. *Patient Care*, Oct. 15, 1993, pp.101-125.

Pannke, Peggy, Long-Term Care Insurance, Directory of Nursing Homes 1991-1992, Oryx Press, 1991, pp.ix-xiii

Pawlson, Dr. L. Gregory, Symposium on Untie the Elderly: Quality Care without Restraints, Serial No. 101-H, U.S. Government Printing Office, 1990, p.70

Pegels, C. Carl, Health Care and the Elderly, Aspen System, Corp., 1981.

Pierce, Robert M., Marshall, Mary A., and Tallon, James R., Jr., Long-Term Care for the Elderly: A Legislator's Guide, National Conference of State Legislatures, Washington, D.C., 1987.

Price, Larry, Workshop on Reducing the Use of Chemical Restraints in Nursing Homes, Serial No. 102-6, U.S. Government Printing Office, 1991, p.55

Rader, Joanne, Symposium on Untie the Elderly: Quality Care without Restraints, Serial No. 101-H, U.S. Government Printing Office, 1990, p.13.

Richards, Marty, Hooyman, Nancy, Hansen, Mary, Brandts, Wendy, Smith-DiJilio, Kathy, and Dahm, Lynn, Choosing a Nursing Home: A Guidebook for Families, University of Washington Press, Seattle, 1984.

Rovner, Barry, W. M.D., et.al., The Prevalence and Management of Dementia and Other Psychiatric Disorders in Nursing Homes. *International Psychogeriatrics 2:* 1990, pp.13-24.

Schneider, Lon S., et al., A metaanalysis of controlled trials of neuroleptic treatment in dementia, *J. Am. Geriatrics Soc.*, 38: 1990, pp.553-563.

Schnelle, J.F., Ouslander, J.G., Osterweil, D. and Blumenthal, S., Total Quality management: Administrative and Clinical Applications in Nursing Homes. *J. Am. Geriatrics Soc.*, 41: 1993, pp.1259-1266.

Shaughnessy, Peter W., Quality of Nursing Home Care, *Generations* Winter,1989, pp.17-20.

Sherman, David S., Psychoactive Drug Misuse in Long-Term Care: Some Contributing Factors. *J. Phamacy Practices* 1:1988, pp.189-194.

Sherman, David S., Workshop on Reducing the Use of Chemical Restraints in Nursing Homes, Serial No. 102-6, U.S. Government Printing Office, 1991, p.4.

Shor, Judi, Changes in Focus for LTC Survey Process, *Contemporary LTC*, May,1984, p.86-7.

Silberfeld, M., Nash, C, and Singer, P.A., Capacity to Complete an Advance Directive, *J. Am. Geriatrics Society*, 41: 1993, pp.1141-1143.

Silverman, Arnold, Symposium on Untie the Elderly: Quality Care without Restraints, Serial No. 101-H, U.S. Government Printing Office, 1990, p.19

Simmons, Mildred, Symposium on Untie the Elderly: Quality Care without Restraints, Serial No. 101-H, U.S. Government Printing Office, 1990, p.13

Simonson, William, Pharm. D., Medications and the Elderly: A Guide for Promoting Proper Use. Aspen Publishing Co.,1984.

Smith, Carol E., DRGs: Making them work for you. *Nursing 85* 15:1985, pp.34-41

Spitx, Bruce, Federal Implementation of OBRA 1987 Nursing Home Reform Provisions, Serial No. 101-4, U.S. Government Printing Office, Washington, D.C., 1990, p.40

Sybert, M. and Weiss, H.P., Gaining the Upper-Hand in the Survey Process, *Contemporary LTC*, Nov.1985, pp.45-48.

Tisdale, Sally, <u>Harvest Moon, Protrait of a Nursing Home</u>, Henry Holt and Co., New York,1987.

Tulloch, G. Janet, From Inside a Nursing Home: A Resident Writes About Autonomy, *Generations*, Supplement, 1990, pp.83-85.

U.S. Department of Health and Human Services, <u>1993 HCFA Statistics</u>, HCFA Press Office, Washington, D.C.,1993.

U.S. House of Representatives Subcommittee on Long Term Care, 96th Congress, <u>Special Problems in Long Term Care</u>, Serial No. 96-208, U.S. Government Printing Office, 1979.

U.S. Senate Committee on Aging, 101st Congress, Workshop on <u>Resident Assessment: The Springboard to Quality of Care and Quality of Life for Nursing Home Residents</u>, Serial No. 101-30, U.S. Government Printing Office, 1991.

U.S. Senate Committee on Aging, 101st Congress. <u>Federal Implementation of OBRA 1987 Nursing Home Reform Provisions.</u> May 18, 1989, p.39.

U.S. Senate Committee on Aging, 102st Congress, Workshop on <u>Reducing the Use of Chemical Restraints in Nursing Homes</u>, Serial No. 102-6, U.S. Government Printing Office, 1991.

U.S. Senate Special Committee on Aging, 101st Congress, <u>Federal Implementation of OBRA 1987 Nursing Home Reform Provisions</u>, Serial No. 101-4, U.S. Government Printing Office, Washington, D.C., 1990.

U.S. Senate Special Committee on Aging, 101st Congress, Symposium on <u>Untie the Elderly: Quality Care without Restraints</u>, Serial No. 101-H, U.S. Government Printing Office, 1990.

Waxman, Hon. Henry A, Congressman from California, Subcommittee on Oversight & Investigations of the Committee on Energy & Commerce. U.S. House of

Representatives, 102nd Congress. Serial No. 102-91, 1992, p.198.

Weaver, Nancy, Group charges deadly neglect in nursing homes. *Sacramento Bee,* Aug. 4, 1994, p.1 and 15.

Weaver, P. & Spiropoulos, J., The Right Way to Choose a Nursing Home, New Team Video, 1991.

Welty, Judy, Workshop on Reducing the Use of Chemical Restraints in Nursing Homes, Serial No. 102-6, U.S. Government Printing Office, 1991, p.29

Whall, L. Ann, Gillis, Lee Grace, Yankou, Dawn, Booth, Dorothy, Beel-Bates, A. Cynthia, Disruptive Behavior in Elderly Nursing Home Residents: A Survey of Nursing Staff. *J. Gerontological Nursing* 18: 1992, pp.13-19.

Williams, Carter Catlett, Long-Term Care and the Human Spirit, *Generations,* Fall,1990, pp.25-28.

Williams, Dr. T. Franklin, Symposium on Untie the Elderly: Quality Care without Restraints, Serial No. 101-H, U.S. Government Printing Office,1990, p.65

Zimmer, James G., MD, Needed: Acute care in the nursing home, *Patient Care,* Nov.1993, pp.59-68.

Zimmerman, David, The Screening Survey, *Generations,* Winter,1989, pp.45-47.

GLOSSARY

Activities of daily living (ADL) -- these includes bathing, dressing eating, grooming, transferring, walking, toileting.

Acute care -- is the around-the-clock skilled nursing care and rehabilitative therapies services for a person having a rapid onset, short coursed, and pronounced symptoms. Medicare, Medicaid, and private insurance companies will cover all of the expenses.

Administrator -- an individual who has had a short term of health administration courses and is responsible for the overall function of the entire facility. All problems stops here.

Agnosia -- unable to recognize familiar faces or objects

Alzheimer's disease -- a degenerative fatal disorder in which brain cells die, and the person progressively loss memory and ADL functions.

Amnesia -- unable to learn new things and is very forgetful.

Anger -- strong feeling of displeasure.

Anti-anxiety drugs --used to treat nervousness and mood changes.

Anti-depressant drugs -- used to treat depression.

Aphasia -- unable to speak or understand language.

Apraxia -- unable to perform the learned motor skills

Benefit period -- the duration of time one is allowed to use services that are covered under Medicare Part A.

Cardiopulmonary resuscitation (CPR) -- a compression and breathing method to assist a person whose heart and breathing had stopped to restart both of those functions again.

Carrier -- a company who has a contract with the federal government to handle durable medical supples or soft goods payments for the Medicare qualified clients in the hospital or at home.

Catastrophe -- a sudden onset of disaster.

Cerebrovascular accident (CVA, stroke) -- the onset of neurological dysfunction resulting from disruption of normal blood supply to the brain. This may be due to a clot or a hemorrhage.

Certified nursing assistants (CNA) -- an individual who has had 150 hours of training and passed the state certification exam to perform direct bedside care of residents in a facility.

Chemical restraints -- any drugs used to control an individual's behavior or moods without any other benefit.

Colostomy bag -- a rubber bag worn as a belt especially constructed to receive the intestinal excretion from the colostomy opening.

Colostomy -- an artificial connection between the large intestine and the surface of the body at the abdominal wall, which is produced by means of surgery.

Convenience -- any action taken by the facility to control resident behavior, or to maintain resident with a lesser amount of effort by the facility, and not necessarily in the resident's best interest.

Custodial care (nursing home, long term care) -- an institution that has a protective environment that provides continuous nursing care and supervision for the incapacitated person in order to meet his or her basic emotional, physical and psychosocial needs.

Delirium -- an acute or subacute change in mental status especially common in the elderly. This condition can be reversed when the underlying causes have been appropriately diagnosed or treated.

Delusional -- false beliefs that other people are stealing from or are trying to hurt an individual.

Dementia -- a syndrome of progressive and irreversible brain dysfunction characterized predominantly by cognitive losses.

Denial --refusal to believe the reality

Dentures -- false teeth.

Department of Health and Human Services (HHS) -- a branch of federal government that sets regulations for various health and human service programs.

Department of Health, Education and Welfare (HEW) -- a branch of federal government that sets regulations for various health, education and welfare programs.

Depression -- an extreme sadness that is unrealistic and out of proportion to any claimed cause.

Diagnosis Related Group (DRG) -- Medicare requirement for setting how many days an individual can stay in the hospital based on a specific disease diagnosis group's guidelines.

Director of nursing (DON) -- a registered nurse who is ultimately responsible for all of the nursing department's functions.

Director of Staff Development (DSD) -- an individual who can be an RN or a LVN whose duties are to teach pre-certification program for nursing assistant, to conduct in-service education for all the staff personnel in the facility, and to supervise the CNAs on the floor.

Discipline -- any action taken by the facility for the sole purpose of punishing or penalizing a resident who exhibited an inappropriate behavior.

Drug toxicity -- any medication taken above a therapeutic level, which leads to developing some unusual signs and symptoms that are harmful or counter-productive to an individual's well being.

Durable medical supplies -- any equipment that is not breakable easily, such as bedside commode, canes, crutches, hospital bed, hoyer lifts, oxygen tank and equipment, wheelchair, and walkers.

Durable power of attorney for finance -- a document that you can use to appoint another person to manage you financial affairs. This usually require an attorney's service.

Durable power of attorney for healthcare -- a document that you can use to appoint another person to make health care decisions for you if you become unable to make that decision on your own.

Dysphagia -- unable to swallow.

Fast-track -- a remedial method imposed by the state licensing and certification division against a troubled facility to extract short-term improvement in the care given to residents.

Gastrotomy tube (G/T) -- a tube inserted directly into the stomach through a small surgical insertion opening to feed a person. This is often safer than using the N/G tube.

Gurney -- a stretcher with wheels for transporting a recumbent (lying down) patient.

Hallucination -- a sensory experience of an object not actually existing in the external world.

Health Care Financing Administration (HCFA) -- a branch of the federal government whose purpose is to oversee all financial and functional aspect of health care programs.

Hemiplegia -- paralysis of one side of the body.

Home health agency -- an agency certified by Medicare regulation to provide nursing services for the client at his/her home. All staff are licensed health professionals. They provide intermittent skilled nursing care, rehabilitation services, and home health aide's service.

Home health aide -- an individual who has had 120 hours of specialized training to care for the client in his/her own home enviornment.

Hypnotic agent -- drugs used for the treatment of sleeplessness.

Ileostomy -- an opening into the small intestine that is created surgically by bringing a part of the small intestine to the outside surface of the body at the abdomen.

Indwelling Foley Catheter -- a tube inserted through the urethra into the bladder to remove urine. The catch bag is usually hung low, under the bed or the chair.

Intermediate care facility (ICF) -- generally serves individual who are ambulatory, continent, requiring minimal assistance and supervision with his/her ADL care.

Intravenous fluid line (IV fluid) -- a tube directly inserted into a vein on back of the hands or in the arm to deliver blood, fluids, or medications.

Leave of absence (LOA) -- an individual who is not on Medicare coverage can leave the facility with a responsible party by getting an LOA.

Licensed Vocational Nurses (LVN) -- an individual who has had short courses of nursing education and is licensed by the state to practice nursing under the supervision of a registered nurse.

Living will -- a legal document in which a person proclaims the desire to be allowed to die a natural death when he is in a state of permanent coma or a life of poor quality that cannot be improved.

Medicaid insurance -- a joint venture of the federal and state government designed to provide financial assistance to low income, poverty stricken population in time of medical need. POE stickers are required for services.

Medicare intermediary -- an organization that has a contract with the federal government to disperse Medicare payments to the hospitals and physicians.

Medicare -- a federal health insurance program administered by the Health Care Financing Administration. It has two parts:

Part A -- a federal health insurance that helps to pay the acute care hospital stay and physician's expenses.

Part B -- helps pay for medically necessary and reasonable physician's services, outpatient services and other medical services and supplies that are not covered by Part A.

Medigap insurance -- when you exhaust your Medicare Part A coverage, this may help to extend coverage for medically necessary covered services in a skilled nursing facility.

Nasal cannula (Oxygen tube) -- a tube with two short rubber prongs inserted into the nostrils to deliver oxygen.

Nasogastric tube (N/G) -- a tube inserted through the nose, the esophagus and into the stomach for supplying nutritional requirement. This tube is sometimes used for an individual who is unable to swallow. This must be checked for displacement before each usage with a stethoscope.

Occupational therapist -- an individual professionally trained in the use of selected occupations for therapeutic purposes. They teach trades and arts as a means of rehabilitation for patients handicapped physically or mentally. They usually concentrate on the fine motor movements of the upper extremities.

Old age assistance (OAA) -- a public assistance program for the elderly that was created in 1935.

Ombudsman -- a nonpartisan public official who investigates people's complaints about government officials and agencies.

Omnibus Budget Reconciliatory Act 1987 (OBRA) -- a law enacted by Congress with comprehensive provisions to regulate the nursing home industry.

Oximeter -- an instrument for the measurement of oxygen concentration in the blood.

Patient care coordinator (PCC) -- an individual who is either a registered nurse or a social worker who has the sole responsibility to work with the family in planning discharge from the acute hospital to home, nursing home or make other arrangement for extension of care.

Pharmacist -- a licensed professional specifically trained to dispense various drugs under the direction and prescription of physicians.

Physical restraint -- any manual method or mechanical device, material, or equipment attached to or adjacent to a resident's body that limits freedom of movement.

Physical therapist -- an individual professionally trained in the utilization of physical agent such as light, heat, cold, water, electricity, message, and exercise for therapeutic purposes. They usually concentrate on gross movement of the lower extremities.

Physician (M. D., Doctor) -- a licensed professional who is authorized to practice medicine.

Posey vest -- a mesh or cloth vest put on the upper torso to prevent a resident from getting up from a chair or falling out of it.

Pre-Admission Screening and Annual Resident Review (PASARR) -- an assessment form for the mentally ill and mentally retarded persons. The use of this assessment is intended to assure more appropriate placement and more appropriate treatment for those mentally ill or mentally retarded who somehow have been inappropriately channeled into nursing homes.

Pressure ulcer -- ulceration of the skin and subcutaneous tissues, due to protein deficiency and prolonged, unrelieved pressure on bony prominence, seen commonly in aged, cachetic, or paralytic bedridden persons.

Psychotropic drugs -- medication used to alter a person's mental function, control behavior or experience. They are primary used to treat mental disorder or illnesses.

Range of motion (ROM) -- In active type, the individual actively participate in the exercise activity with minimal assistance, while in passive exercises, the nurse or the therapist does the exercise for an individual. The range of motion exercises are designed to flex all the joints of the body in order to prevent contraction and weakness of the muscles.

Registered nurse (RN) -- a professional individual who has had more than two, three or four years of nursing training and is licensed by the board of nursing to practice nursing under the Nursing Practice Act.

Reserved days -- Medicare benefit will give you only 60 reserve days in your lifetime. These benefit days can be used in any of the allowed Medicare service categories.

Resident Assessment Instrument (RAI) -- the primary screening and assessment tool of residents in a nursing home. It provides information about an individual's strengths, weaknesses, needs and preferences.

Resident Assessment Protocols (triggers, and RAPS) -- provide the crucial problem identification link between assessment and the development of care plan goals. The definitions that trigger the RAP conditions refer to particular MDS items or combination of items that an individual may require care plan intervention.

Resident rights -- each individual admitted to a nursing home has twenty-two guaranteed rights which protect them from abuses and neglect of quality of life and quality of care.

Residential care -- facility that provides safe, clean, and sheltered living to individual capable of functional independence. They stress the social needs rather than medical needs.

Skilled nursing facility (rehabilitation unit, subacute unit) -- an institution that is licensed to participate in Medicare and Medicaid programs, meets the National Fire Protection Association Life Safety Code and federal regulations for long-term care facilities, and meet state licensure requirements. It is a distinct part of a convalescent hospital. The primary purpose of this component is to provide intensive skilled nursing care services and rehabilitative therapies for the convalescing of injuried, disabled individual.

Social worker -- a skilled, professional individual who provides counselling, emotional support, activity, organized and directed which seeks to help individuals or groups through their environmental situation.

Speech pathologist -- a specialist dealing with disorders of speech and language.

Speech therapist -- a specialist dealing with dysfunctions of the vocal cord and the swallowing reflex.

Utilization Review Committee (URC) -- is made up of the administration personnel of the facility, physicians, rehabilitative team personnel and pharmacist The committee meets once a month to review the criteria and qualification of a patient based on the status for Medicare coverage.

RESOURCES

This is only a partial list of available senior resources. There are hundreds of senior citizens' organizations, and resource books and magazines are on the market or in the libraries.

American Association of Homes for the Aging (a non-profit agency)
1050 17th St, NW
Suite 770
Washington, DC 20036

American Association of Retired Persons
601 E St, NW
Washington, DC 20049

American Health Care Association (for profit)
Long Term Care Survey, The
Regulation, Forms, Procedures, and Guidelines
1201 L street, NW
Washington, DC 20005-4014

American Society on Aging
Aging Today (newspaper)
833 Market Street.
Suite 511
San Francisco, CA 94103-1824

Area 4 on Aging
Office on Aging
455 Capital Mall
Suite 500
Sacramento, CA 95814

Area Agency on Aging
National Headquarters
Suite 400
1828 L St.
Washington, DC 20036

California Association of Health Facilities (CAHF)
Regional Office
3225 Wilshire Blvd
Suite 625
Los Angeles, CA 90010
(213) 380-7715

California Partnership Insurance in Long Term Care
California Department of Aging
LTC Information Line
1337 Braden Court
P.O. Box 1028
Orange, CA 92688-1028
     For questions on whether an agent is authorized to sell long term care insurance, call 1-800-927-4357
     To obtain a list of private insurance companies that sell these policies, call 1-800-434-0222.

Geriatric Nursing
Mosby-Year Book Inc.
11830 Westline Industrial Dr.,
St. Louis, MO 63146-3318

HCFA, Office of Survey and Certification
    for Resident Assessment Instrument Training Manual
Director, Division of Long Term Care Services
Meadows East Building- Area 2-D2
6325 Security Blvd.
Baltimore, MD. 21202
Atten: Nursing Home Branch
    All nursing facility has a copy of this manual.
    Suggestion for improving the training manual should
    be directed to the above address.

Health Insurance for People With Medicare, 1995 Guide to,
1 (800) 638-6833

Journal of Gerontological Nursing (topics on nursing care of
older adults)
Slack Incorporated
6900 Grove Road
Thorofare, NJ 08086
(609) 848-1000

National Association of Home Health Agency
426 C. St. N.E.,
Washington, DC 20002

National Committee to Perserve Social Security and
Medicare
    for the magazine *Secure Retirement*--
2000 K.St. N.W.
Suite 800
Washington, DC 20006
(202) 822-9459.

National Council for Homemakers Services, Inc.
67 Irving Place
New York, NY10003

National Council on the Aging
1828 L St. NW
Washington, DC 20026.

National Eldercare Institute (on elder abuse and state long-term care Ombudsman services
2033 K. St. N.W.
Suite 304
Washington, DC 20006

Nursing Magazine
Springhouse Corporation
1111 Bethleham Pike,
Springhouse, PA 19477
(215) 646-8700

Office of Nursing Home Affairs
5600 Fisher's Lane
Room 17B-07
Rockville, MD 20852.

Peter Weaver and John Spiropoulous
How to Stretch Your Retirement Dollars
47 minute video, 116 pages book
1 800 852-1355

Senior Magazine - Capitol City edition
900 Fulton Ave. Suite 103
Sacramento, CA 95825
1 (800) 200-7707
Fax (916) 972-0825

Senior Chronicle
PO Box 19199
Sacramento, CA 95829
(916) 452-4023
Fax (916) 452-3606.

United Senior Health Cooperation
1331 H. St. N.W.
Suite 800
Washington, DC. 20006

U.S. Administration on Aging
300 Independence Ave, SW
Washington, DC 20201

U. S. Senate Subcommittee on Long-Term Care
Special Committee on Aging
Room 3121
Dirksen Senate Office Building
Washington, DC 20510
        or
U. S. Government Printing Office
Superintendent of Documents
Congressional Sales Office,
Washington, DC 20402

220

INDEX

abuse 16, 170
acceptance 7
accountant 94
Activities Director 43
activities of daily living (ADL)
    25, 32, 118
activity pursuit patterns 27
Administrator 40
admission agreement 60
admission inquiry 58
admission policy 63
admission procedure 65
agnosia 137
AIDS residents 21
Alzheimer residents 21
Alzheimer's disease 137
amnesia 137
anger 6
antianxiety drugs 143
antidepressant drugs 143
anxiety 139
aphasia 137
apraxia 137
attached harness 163
attitude of the management
    team 48

bargain 6
bathing stool 8
bathroom 50
bed-hold policy 56, 74
bedside commode 8
bedside rails 163
bedside rails consent 72
bedside slings 163
bedsores 28, 121
behavior 27
benefit period 78

Board of Directors 36
bowel and bladder 18

California Partnership for Long-
    Term Care 94
call bell 52, 119
care plan 29
caregiver 8
cerebrovascular accident (CVA)
    2, 26
Certified Nursing Assistant
    (CNA) 33, 42, 53, 54, 173
change of condition 128
chemical restraints 28, 134ff
chronically ill 32, 33
citizenship 105
clothing 112
CNA training 173
Cognitive loss 25
communication 25
comprehensive assessment 22
confusion 9
consent to medication and
    treatment 67
consultant pressure 184
convalescent hospital 4, 19, 31,
    46
Convenience 136
corporate managed nursing
    home 36
cost 45
coverage in skilled nursing
    homes 79
CPR status 68
custodial care 18, 80

daily basis 80
decision inputs 162

decubitus 28, 121
deficient knowledge 190
dehydration 28
delirium 24, 136
delusional 138
dementia 25, 137
denial 6
dental care 28
Department of Health,
        Education and Welfare
        17
Department of Social Welfare 46
depression 7, 138
Diagnosis Related Group (DRG)
        3, 4
Dietary Supervisor 43
dignity 98
Director of Activities 55
Director of Nursing (DON) 32,
        37, 39, 41, 59, 183
Director of Social Services 55
Director of Staff Development
(DSD) 42, 54, 178
disabled elderly 32
discharge planning 3, 6
disciplinary action 177
discipline 135
disorientation 9
drug toxicity 140
durable powerof attorney for
        health care 71

emotional deterioration 160
entitlement balance 110
environment 116
evaluation of resident for
        physical restraint 164
extended care 80
extended care facility 17
external catheter 26

facility denial 84
facility licensing number 49

fall prevention 156, 165
falls 27
family council 55, 107
family doctor 2
family physician 10
feeding tube 27
financial planner 94
fluid maintenance 28
free enterprise 171
furnishings 112

garbled speech 9
general appearance 48
geri-chair 51
go low and go slow 146

hallucination 138
Health Care Facilities
        Administration
        (HCFA) 19
hearing 121
hearing patterns 25
home care 10
home health agencies (HHA) 4,
        9
home health aides 10
homemaker agencies 10
hospital bed 8
housekeeping 43
hydration 127
hypnotic agents 144

inadequate financial resources
        46
inadequate training 190
incompatibility factor 177
incontinence 9, 26
independent contractors 130
individual wishes 103
individually and family owned
        37
infection control 132
initial impression 48

inspecting team 30
inspector's survey 49
institutional rules 103
intensive care unit 2
interdisciplinary team 22
intermediate care facilities 18, 34
intravenous fluid therapy 21
involvement of individual
    resident 62

lap belt 162
laundry services 115
Laundry Supervisor 43
leave of absence 74
Licensed Vocational Nurses
    (LVN) 18, 32, 41, 53, 179
living will 71
location of the facility 47
long-term care 13, 14, 80
long-term care facility 32
long-term disability 14
low-income beneficiaries 88

mail 111
maintenance supervisor 43
mandated postings 49
meal time 52
Medicaid 5, 15, 17, 18, 90
Medicaid certification 91
Medicaid coverage 91
Medicaid reimbursement 46,
    171, 191
Medicaid resident 92
Medicaid-supported 171
Medical Director 85
Medical Records Clerk 42
medical records 38
Medical Social Worker 10, 22
medical/rehabilitation aspect 48
Medicare 5, 9, 17, 18, 19, 77
Medicare Intermediary denial
    86
Medicare Part A 33, 78, 79

Medicare PART B 78, 87
Medicare payment 82
Medicare unit 20
medication errors131
Medigap insurance 79
Medigap Supplement 81
mental impairment 139
middle or working class 76
Minimum Data Set (MDS) 22,
    24, 117, 134
misuse 146
mood patterns 26
nasogastric/gastrostomy
    feeding 124
neglect 16
"NO" to CPR 70
non-covered services 87
non-discriminatory policies 64
non-profit or not-for-profit
    facilities 39
non-skid strips 8
nurse consultant 39
nursing assistants 18
nursing department problems
    172
nursing home 4, 10, 15, 18
nursing home care expenses 76
nutrition 126
nutritional status 27

OBRA regulations 117
occupational therapist 22, 83
occupational therapy 10
Office Manager 42
office politics 185
Old Age Assistance (OAA) 16
Ombudsman 46
Omnibus Budget Reconciliation
    Act (OBRA 1987) 19, 53,
    98, 171
"on-call" list 179
operational philosophy 172
out of standards 171

over-medication 149, 150
ownership 31, 35

Partnership Insurance in Long-
   Term Care 94
Patient Care Coordinator (PCC)
   4, 59
patient/facility policies and
   procedures 61
pelvic crotch restraint 163
personal attending physician
   105
personal care 35
personal possessions 112
personal properties 55
pharmacy 72, 130
pharmacy consultant 148
physical and chemical restraint
   72
physical function 25
physical illnesses 140
physical restraint 155
physical restraints 28, 52, 155ff
physical therapist 22, 33, 83
physical therapy 10
physician 41, 188
planned activities 55
planning care and treatment 106
poorhouse 16
posey vest 162
preferred intensity of care 68
pressure sores 28
pressure ulcers 121
primary care physician 22
privacy and dignity 120
private funds 110
private insurance 19, 92
private insurance payments 93
private nursing care 35
private physician 46
private-paying 45
Professional Service Specialist
   (PSS) 37

Professional Services Consultant
   (PSC) 37
proprietorship 35
psychosocial aspect 55
psychosocial deterioration 160
psychosocial well-being 26
psychotropic drug 28
psychotropic Drugs 141

quality of care 18, 117ff
quality of life 97ff

range of motion 124
re-admission 74
reduction of restraints   167
registered nurse (RN) 9, 32, 33,
   41, 53
rehabilitation 9
rehabilitation aide 22, 33
rehabilitation potential 25
rehabilitation service 21, 81, 83
reserve days 79
resident abuse 175
resident and family groups 107
Resident Assessment
   Instrument (RAI) 21
Resident Assessment Protocol
   Summary (RAPS) 23, 24
Resident Assessment Protocol
   Worksheet 23
resident council 55, 107
residential care facility 34
restraint consent form 163
right to choose 109
right to privacy 111
roll bar 163
roommate 11, 56
routine medications 131

safety bar 8
self-autonomy 22
self-control 22
self-determination and

participation 99
self-dignity and respect 22
sheet tucked 163
side effects 144
skilled nursing care 81
skilled nursing facility (SNF) 5,
    19, 31, 33
skilled nursing services 82
smoking guidelines 113
Smoking policies 56
Social Security Act 17
Social Service Director 43
social services 113
special needs 129
speech therapist 22, 83
speech therapy 10
spending down 90
staff shortage 176
staffing adequacy 53, 184
stages of pressure sore 122
straight insurance policy 93
sub-acute unit 20
Supervisor 32, 182

tardive dyskinesia 144
target behaviors 145
tax lawyer 94
telephone 111
the revolving door policy 177
the tell-tale signs 50
theft and losses 114
tracheotomy care and
suctioning 21
transfer 73
transfer procedures 62
trapeze 8
triggers 23
types of physical restraints 162
urinary incontenence 123
Utilization Review Committee
    (URC) 85
Utilization Review Committee
    denial 85

ventilator management 21
violations 153
visions 121
vision patterns 25
visits and visitors 108

walker 8
wheelchair 8, 51
wrist restraints 163
written communication 111

Questions & Answers about
"How to Achieve Quality Of Life & Care In a Nursing Home"

1. You are a practitioner in the field of nursing and social works, what made you decide to write a book of this type?

A. I have worked for many years in all different capacities in nursing homes. I have interacted with residents, families, physicians and the staff. I have seen all of the problems, the patchwork solutions, the frustrations and the wishful thinking. I am an optimist. I think things can be better particularly if the families know really what goes on there and what rights do they have. That is why I decided to write this book.

2. You mention this or allude to the fact that nursing home has not been, nor is it currently a very healthy environment for the patient (or resident). Are there any hopes of their becoming better?

A. Yes, when families of the residents are armed with real knowledge of the regulations governing these facilities, when they are not being intimidated or led astray by the staff or administration, then they can start to push for the real changes for the better. That means attaining and maintaining physical,
emotional, psychosocial and spiritual well-being.

3. One of the initial questions anyone faces in such a situation as you depict in Chapter 1 is: Aren't there better alternatives? How do you compare the options?

A. Yes, there are. However, everything has its trade-offs. You have the Home Health Agencies, but they cover basically only Medicare covered services. Once the coverage stops, the cost is prohibitively high. You have the Home Care agencies. They don't do any nursing care at all. If you do home care yourself, then your own quality of life will suffer significantly.

4. You mention over and over again this OBRA 1987 as if it were some great innovation from the Feds. How good is it? Do they really know it is the right approach? Why does this one regulation have hope for the future resident?

A. OBRA 1987 did not come out of the vacuum. It is the result of many studies and special sessions of the congressional committees. The major differences between this regulation and those previous ones are two: (1) This is a total person approach. The resident is being assessed in toto by a broad-based interdisciplinary team of health and social experts. This approach is not disease oriented as the acute hospital focus. Its focus is psychosocial. 2) The regulation carries with it a stiff enforcement arm. Once there are citations, Medicare and Medicaid funding can be withheld.

5. There are several terminologies for the nursing home. Do they differ much one from another?

A. Really there are only two types: The custodial care type which can be called the nursing home, the convalescent hospital or a long-term care facility, is one group. The other is the truly
skilled nursing facility (SNF) which resembles a subacute unit of a hospital. Unfortunately, many SNFs are also called one of those other terms, and many custodial care facilities have a small SNF unit, hence enabling them to call themselves a SNF/convalescent hospitals.

6. Can any lay person really get a good sense of quality assessment in a single visit to a prospective nursing home?

A. Yes. What you have to do is to really use your own five senses: sight, sound, smell, taste, and touch. Then these have to be supplemented by the Inspectors Reports. A good grasp of what I have mentioned in the Choosing chapter would also help.

7. Admission to a regular hospital is often a big pain. How, if so, does the admission process into a nursing home differ?

A. Admission into the nursing home requires much paper work. Since sometimes this will be their home for a long time, there are many pieces of documents to sign. It takes at least two hours to read thoroughly this material before actually signing them.

8. You have mentioned quality of care and life of a resident. Would the family of a nursing home resident have to be there 24 hours a day to insure that the high quality is practiced? At what stage can I let go a little and be assured of continued quality?

A. If you work positively with the staff, showing your concern and knowledge, there will be positive feedback in the care. If you have difficulty with the line staff, get above them to the Director of Nursing, the Administrator, or the Social Service Director. Then there is the Ombudsman and finally the state inspectors. No facility likes to have inspectors on its back. They will do something to correct the problem. Another place to bring up the problems of a more general nature is the Family Council or the Resident Council.

9.   The same goes for these unethical and illegal use of restraints, either physical or chemical. How does one know that something is not being practiced behind our backs?

A.   The illegal use of these restraints could mean life and death of a resident. There should be zero tolerance by you as a family member. Knowing the regulations clearly yourself would set the right tone in dealing with the staff on these matters. That is why I spent two chapters dealing with these topics.

10.   Besides being a hawk over our individual loved one, are there any class action type of efforts that will tend to improve the overall trend of nursing home care?

A.   When paper compliance becomes the rule, it is time to take some concerted action. First, there is simply too much paperwork required of the staff in a nursing home. You can help by writing to your congressmen and demanding true resident care time and assessment instead of paper compliance. The other major problem in the nursing home is the lack of funding. This precipitates minimal staffing, low wages, overworked staff members, and unappreciated efforts. You have to ask yourself if a dignified existence as a resident in a nursing home is a right of our seniors? If so, the programs that fund this function must be adequately supported. Again, political decisions will require grassroots support.   There is something skewed in our value system when the Medicaid funding for a day of nursing home stay is lower than what a night in a standard motel room might cost.

11.   What is the difference between your book and all other books about nursing homes that are on the market or bookshelves?

Each book presents a different perspective. In order to get a good picture of this topic, the nursing home life and the industry behind it, many perspectives are needed. My book is written based on my personal experience working in many nursing homes. I have some in-depth insights of how nursing homes function and why they are what they are. I share with many other writers with the opinion that individual care givers are often very caring and dedicated. However, from what I have seen and experienced, I also know where the problems are. Staff shortage is real. Too top heavy and not enough workers is often real. Lack of support from the administration is sadly also often true. I try to address all of these problems and come up with possible solutions.

12. You mention in the Addendum that from a very recent workshop (June 29 & 30, 1995), new enforcement teeth have been built into the new OBRA for enforcement of regulations. Do you think the quality of life and quality of care will really improve?

Because the regulations allow state inspectors to categorize facilities as good or bad, and such categorization is open information, the facility administration must be somewhat sensitive to which category it is in. Just by that sense of knowledge, and the fear that getting into the bad category takes a lot of effort to get back out, these facilities will strive to simply stay out of the bad category. It is simply a case of economics: If branded as bad, and it is public knowledge, that facility will lose residents, or at least not gain any new residents.

13. Where can I get such information about a particular facility? Suppose I want to have inspectors reports from three previous years.

Each state has its own department of health and human services. They may have different names, but the function is the same. Look under this department and get the division of licensing and certification. They can provide you with detailed information about any facility you might want to know. This is public information and should be completely accessible.

14. Where can I obtain a list of Residents Rights?

In the same division, there should be a published list of Residents Rights for public distribution. In the state of California, the California Association of Healthcare Facilities (CAHF) also keeps copies of these Residents Rights for public distribution.

15. If I represent my loved one who is living in one of these facilities and demand that certain specific rights be given to him or her, might I not expect some form of facility retaliation?

No one in any facility is ever allowed to retaliate against a specific resident. That too is a very serious violation if retaliation indeed took place and is proven. I mention in my book that facilities really appreciate an informed and concerned public. They become the eyes and ears of the facilities in the same manner that the CNAs are supposed to be. The best situation would be to have the facility administration, the nursing staff and the concerned public all work as a team to keep the facility in that good category.

16. I am realistic enough to know that there always will be some bad staff member among the many caring individuals. If I do find neglect and/or abuse, what can I do?

First of all, any employee who is caught or has been reported to be abusive towards a resident will be investigated by the administration immediately. If the situation is found to be true, the employee is terminated immediately, and the incident is duly reported to the department of health services, to its licensing and certification division. The state can conduct its own investigation and can cite the facility if the result of the abuse is serious.

17. Suppose the CNA assigned to my loved one is very busy. How can I get the attention of him/her for attending to my loved ones needs?

Nursing assistants are taught that they must respond to the call bell within 3-5 minutes after it has been rung. In fact, any staff member in the facility who sees the call light first must answer it first. After assessing the situation that brought on the call bell (light), they can then go and get thee assigned aide to handle the situation. If the particular assigned aide is off the floor at that time (for break or meals), another one is always assigned to be the relief aide. Just ask the charge nurse or the supervisor for the assignment list.

18. How often does the physician visit residents in a nursing home?

This answer depends on whether the resident is in the custodial care segment of the nursing home or in the sub-acute care unit (skilled nursing unit). For custodial care residents, the physician is only required to see him/her once a month. This is because under Medicaid, physicians are paid for only one visit per month. For those in the skilled nursing units, care by the physician may be on a daily basis, depending on the severity of the case, for only one visit peer

232

month. For those in the skilled nursing units, care by the physician may be on a daily basis, depending on the severity of the case.

19. What can I do if my loved one lost some of his/her belongings?

I go into this topic in some detail in the book because this loss certainly will affect the quality of life of that resident. The chief person to contact is the Director of Social Services. This individual will then assess as to whether the loss is the result of nursing department action or the result of other departments actions, for instance the laundry or the activities department. Appropriate responsible personnel then will be brought into the investigation. It is probably safe to say that personal belongings are more often mishandled and/or misplaced than stolen. For instance, unlabeled clothing can get misplaced by the laundry personnel after washing. Unmarked glasses may be misplaced by a resident while in the activity room. There are ways to make these belongings less likely to be misplaced. Marking them clearly with the residents name is a good start.

20. What is the profile of the typical resident in a nursing home?

Predominantly they are white, middle-class, female between the age of 75 to 85 or even older. Most are widowed and have some children who look after their welfare while they reside in the facility. They generally have some ailment that made them difficult to impossible to be cared for in the home of a daughter or son. This may be either physical handicap resulting from old age or medical illness or mental problem again resulting from aging or serious illness such as stroke or Alzheimer. More than 50% are on Medicaid because they have spent down to their last $2000 of personal assets. There are also the short-term patient/residents of the sub-acute unit (skilled nursing unit). These may be anyone who finds that there is a need of some rehabilitation after an acute illness prior to returning home.

21. Why should a young person be attracted to this book?

A: The topic discussed here actually transcends age boundaries. One obvious reason is that this young person may be the significant family member who is taking care of his/her parents or grandparents, who need the nursing home care. Secondly, a young person may know a friend who has to face such a choice either for him/herself or for his/her relatives.   Beyond that, even though many young people think of themselves as invincible, they are often the victims of accidents, violent crimes and other unforeseen, debilitating injuries or illnesses. Any of these can incapacitate them for a long duration. Once that happens, the long-term disability could cause severe strains in their support structure and financial resources; then they may have to consider entering a nursing home. Let us consider several concrete examples: Say a young man has been seriously injured in an automobile or motorcycle accident. He cannot afford to pay high enough wages for a home-maker to come to his own home to tend to his needs. If he has no other support system to back him up, then he may have to consider nursing home rehabilitation. As another example, there are indeed young stroke or brain tumor victims who have been rendered incontinent of bowel and bladder and who require significant assistance in two or more activities of daily living. When the family members are completely exhausted, there is a good chance that he/she will end up in a nursing home for

234

sustained, professional care.

For students of parents with a low or lowest income

"HOW TO OBTAIN MAXIMUM COLLEGE FINANCIAL AID"

The financial aid counselor's job is to make sure the student doesn't get too much money. The student's job is to make sure he/she gets the maximum amount from the Governmental Aid Program. To do this, one must know how the answers to the questions on the Financial Aid Form impact the awards. This information is in this book.

* COLLEGE FINANCIAL AID is an involved process. This book makes the steps clear and understandable.

* the book clarifies the questions on the Financial Aid Form.

* the book shows with sample situations how the answers to the questions on the form impact the amount of your award. This understanding allows the student and/or family to arrange their assets and income as to maximize their awards.

* the book describes many different governmental awards.

* See how to 1) finance correspondence courses, remedial courses & foreign study 2) use the new loan repayment plans to avoid defaulting 3) choose a proprietary school properly 4) have maximally assured employment after graduation 5) locate non-governmental loaning sources etc.

Student College Aid Publishing, 7950 N Stadium Dr #229 Houston, 77030 1-(800) 245-5137 * 5.5" X 8.5" Pprback 178 pgs $12.95 + $3 Postage Satisfaction guaranteed! We accept personal check, Visa or MC.

A perfect gift for someone whose education you care about!

a gift for students in college or going to college

"LESS COMPETITIVE COLLEGE GRANTS & LOANS
NEW EXPANDED SECOND EDITION"

In searching for awards the idea is to find those awards that are less competitive. Your odds for getting money from these awards are greater. Most students overlook these preferential sources of college money. Be your own advocate. Find your proper awards in this book.

The most important step is to apply. But where to apply? Apply where there is less competition and more favoritism. You will qualify to apply for these awards by your place of residence or your anticipated college major(s). This makes finding your sources easy. But don't forget, if you get turned down, apply again the next application period. Persistence pays off.

Enumerated are private foundations giving money to college students or college bound high school students. Some awards are for a few hundred dollars; others are for thousands.

This book lists the name of the award, requirements to qualify, when to apply, name and address of your contact. Updating of book was done by phone or fax in order to not allow data to become outdated.

There are about 1500 different listings in this book. It's a perfect gift for someone whose education you care about!

Student College Aid, Publishing Div., 7950 N. Stadium Dr. #229 · Houston, TX 77030 1-(800) 245-5137 · FAX (713) 796-9963. 6 X 9 paperback 352 pages Price $16.99 plus $3.00 postage. Satisfaction guaranteed! We accept personal check, Visa or MC.

"DIRECTORY OF COLLEGE ALUMNI GROUPS"

Students don't realize that alumni establish many scholarships for entering students. This is how the "Directory of College Alumni Groups" is used.

Suppose a student from Houston wants to go to Williams College in Massachusetts. He/she looks up the alumni phone number under the college name, calls and requests a phone number for the president of the nearest chapter. The president is contacted, the student's desire to attend Williams is expressed. The president sets up a personal meeting with a member of the alumni club and the student. If that interview goes well the group can help the student gain admittance and financial aid.

The catalogs of the alumni awards is not printed for general distribution. The purpose of this directory is also to aid the student in finding these awards. As a college education becomes ever more difficult to finance, alumni groups become increasingly important.

Student College Aid, Publishing, 7950 N. Stadium Dr. #229, Houston, 77030 1-(800) 245-5137 · 6 X 9 pprback 352 pgs $9.95 + $3.00 postage. Satisfaction guaranteed! We accept personal check, Visa or MC.

A perfect gift for someone whose education
you care about!

Elizabeth Yeh was born in Beijing, China and spent her formative years in China during World War II. Her grandmother taught her to always help others, pay heed to the wisdom of the elders, respect them for their knowledge, and have faith in God. In those years she witnessed war atrocities and suffering among her neighbors, relatives, and friends. It was then she decided to help people when she grew up.

She and her mother immigrated to the United States in 1952. She could not read, speak or understand English. A dedicated and empa- thetic social worker saw that Elizabeth was enrolled in the School for Immigrants in Boston, MA. There she learned to read, speak, write, and understand English from the kindergarten level through the 9th grade. Then she transferred to St. Anne's School in Arlington Heights, MA. Her grandmother's advice was reinforced by the Episcopalian Sisters. Her desire to help people grew even stronger as she grew older. She volunteered to work for the American Red Cross and worked as a nurse's aide in an acute hospital. After high school, she entered nursing school at Brigham and Women's Hospital (formerly the Peter Bent Brigham Hospital School of Nursing), which is affiliated with Harvard Medical School. Upon receiving her diploma and RN license in 1959, she attended Boston College School of Nursing and obtained her Bachelor of Science degree in Nursing in 1961.

Her husband is a graduate of MIT. They have two daughters; one is an MD; the other is a paralegal.

Early on Elizabeth worked part-time in an acute hospital and in an out-patient clinic. She was instrumental in helping start a free dental program for the children in the public school system of a poor district. While working she realized that nursing skills and knowledge alone are not enough to help people, because there are other needs that affect their health. So she returned to California State University-Sacramento and obtained in 1975 a degree in Master of Social Welfare with a concentration in health planning, policies and administration. While working as a home health agency's discharge planner operating in local skilled nursing facilities, her best friend asked her to become the Director of Nursing for one of her facilities. Since then she has worked in a variety of positions in SNFs, as Director of Nursing, as Director of Staff Development, as Supervisor, and as a treatment nurse. She saw the frustration residents and their families felt with the administration. Most of them felt helpless because they were not aware they had all types of rights and resource people to help them in solving their problems. It was with this in mind that she decided to write this book. Her primary objective is to provide people with an informative guide to refer to when the need for a nursing home arises.

NOTES

NOTES

NOTES

NOTES

NOTES

NOTES

NOTES